Grief Changed Me

A Widows Heartbeat

Delilah Klug

DEDICATION

For the widows who wake up each day unsure how to keep going—
and keep going anyway.

For those who lost the love of their life
and had to rebuild a world from the ashes.

For every woman who found herself
in the ruins,
and rose.

CONTENTS

ACKNOWLEDGMENTS

To Dustin—love didn't end. It changed shape and kept beating through me. Your heartbeat still echoes in the way I mother, write, and rise. I carry you in every page.

To my children—thank you for giving me reasons to keep going. You are my why, my proof that love and legacy can survive the fire.

And to the woman I became in the ruins—thank you for staying. For choosing life when nothing about it felt fair. You are not the afterthought of a tragedy. You are the author of what comes next.

.

Before You Step Into These Pages

This book is different.
It's deeper.
Heavier.

This isn't just about grief anymore—
it's about the aftermath.
The fire.
The silence.
The survival.

These pages hold truths I wasn't ready to write the first time,
when I was still healing parts of my soul.
But I'm ready now.
And if you're holding this book,
I believe you're ready to read it.

You won't find fluff here.
You won't find shallow comfort or easy answers.
What you will find
is a woman who has lived through the unimaginable—
and wrote her way through it anyway.

This book carries love and it carries anger,
because grief is both.
Don't mistake my anger for hate—
it's what happens when pain is multiplied by betrayal.

This book may feel heavy at times—
because it carries the weight of love,
loss,
motherhood,
betrayal,
and the sacred work of rising again.

If you need to pause, pause.
If you need to cry, let those tears fall.
But please know this:

You are not alone here.
And you are not broken for feeling every word.

This isn't the beginning of a story.
It's the continuation of a heartbeat
that refuses to stop.

"I didn't just survive the fire. I became someone new inside it."
—Delilah Klug

1 Becoming Her Without Him

PART 1 — The Day Everything Ended

I never expected to be here.
But here I am—
a woman rewritten by loss.

Still breathing.
Still mothering.
Still holding on to a love
I can no longer touch.

I didn't know how much grief would take—
how much of me I'd lose
just trying to survive it.

I didn't know there would be a day—
a dividing line
between the life I knew
and the one I never asked for.

One breath—
and everything changed.

The air felt different.
He was gone.
And I was still here.

People talk about keeping small things after someone dies—
a scent,
a pillow,
anything to hold onto when you can't bear the emptiness.

But what if the fire took everything?

In the beginning, I was numb—without a doubt.
Widow's brain fog blanketed every memory,
every thought,
every feeling I had left.

I wasn't still in the house,
but every decision felt like walking through smoke—
trying to see clearly,
trying to find a way out to safety.

What if you were left
with nothing but memory
and the sound of your own scream
echoing through the chaos?

But it wasn't just him I lost.
It was the home we built in this world.

The walls that held our memories.
The floors where our babies crawled.
The kitchen where laughter echoed.

It all went up in flames—
in the same cruel moment
I lost the man I loved.

I lost the future we were building,
and in the wreckage,
I lost pieces of myself—
pieces that I may never fully get back.

I'm not just grieving him.
I'm grieving the version of me
who once felt loved unconditionally,
held,
protected,
safe.

Grief doesn't just break your heart.
it hands you the paperwork.

It forces you to become an administrator
of your own devastation.

Not only mourning them,
but dismantling the life
you built with them
piece by painful piece.

The sharp, unexpected weight followed:
removing his name from accounts,
changing documents,
making phone calls no one should ever have to make.

Sitting on hold with customer service,
repeating the words,
"My husband passed away,"
as if speaking it aloud made it more real.

Each call felt like another goodbye.
Another way to separate what once was
from what is now.

People talk about picking up the pieces.
But what do you do
when the pieces are ashes?

It's strange,
how something as sacred as loss
gets reduced to a form—
proof required
just to change a number.

It wasn't just paperwork.
It was heartbreak
on repeat.

But I did it.
Even when my voice shook.
Even when my hands trembled.
Even when the silence after the call
felt louder than the grief itself.

Because I had to.

Because no one else stayed after the smoke and embers.

They left before the real aftermath began—
before my soul had time to grasp reality.
Before I could even feel the weight of my tragic loss.

I was left in the crushing moments
of trying to survive
minute by minute.

There was no future in sight
in those earlier months.

Because when survival takes over,
everything else—
dreams,
passions,
future plans—
feels out of reach, those all laid with my husband.

I didn't know what came next.
How could I?

I was trapped in my body—
an empty walking vessel
just trying to make sense
of what the hell just happened.

Where's my husband?
Where are my kids?
My heart?

What do you mean we no longer have a home to return to?
What do you mean he's never coming back?
What am I supposed to do now?

My life once held
with both hands—
and now I'm just trying not to drop
the pieces that are still left.

And in doing so,
I became her—
the woman who carries it all.

Sometimes,
it wasn't the big,
life-altering moments
that brought me to my knees—

it was the small,
soul-crushing ones.

A phone call.
A form.
A final signature
that made it official.

And somehow,
after all that undoing,
life still expected me
to keep showing up.

Some days,
even something as simple
as ordering a holiday shirt
was enough to wreck me.

One popped up online—
the kind he would've loved.

And just like that,
I was back in the ache.
Back in the memory
of matching Fourth of July shirts,
of him laughing
in red, white, and blue.

It's the kind of grief
that sneaks in
through the everyday moments.

And still,
I kept going.

I remember the first time
I hugged my kids
after the fire.

It was days later—
the breathing tube
had just been removed.

I was dazed,
medicated,
confused…
still recovering
from the kind of trauma
that tries to take everything.

But when I reached out,
my kids fell into me.
And I did the same.

We just held each other,
refusing to let go.

That hug said everything
words couldn't—
the fear,
the love,
the loss,
the relief.

It whispered,
"You still have me."
Even if everything else has changed.

We were grieving
as a family—
confused,
heartbroken,
raw.

That moment held
the weight of their father,
and the weight
of what we had just survived.

It was the first moment we knew:
we were still here.
Together.

But never the same.

It's strange
how life keeps asking you
to do the impossible—
not all at once,
but in a thousand quiet tasks
that feel like grief in disguise.

You don't just lose your person.
You lose the rhythm
of your days.

The shared glances.
The silent teamwork.
The way they knew
what you needed
before you even said a word.

Your shared dreams,
your parenting,
your growth—
it was never about just you.

It was for the whole.
The us.
The family.

The future you had built
with someone you never expected
to live without.

What goals did I have
when all the goals I once craved
I laid to rest
with my husband?

And when all of that is gone,
you're left holding decisions
you never wanted to make—

in a world
that doesn't pause
for your pain.

Because even after loss—
even after everything—
the world doesn't slow down.

But I did.

I slowed down enough
to notice
what still mattered.

To hold onto pieces of him
in the everyday moments.

Stillness
is strength,
too.

Sometimes
I look back and wonder
how I survived
any of it.

The loss.
The fire.

Life about took me out—
just trying to survive.
Over and over again.

And the truth is,
there were moments
it almost did.

But even in the darkest hours,
something in me held on.

A whisper.
A thread.
A heartbeat.

I didn't survive
because I was strong.
I survived
because I didn't stop.

You've walked through hell
with nothing but your heartbeat
and a fierce kind of love
holding you together.

And still—
you're here.

Not untouched.
Not unchanged.
But here.

That's not just survival.
That's defiance.
That's devotion.
That's you.

You have every right
to sit in this moment—
and feel all of it.

The weight.
The ache.
The sacred shock
of still being here,
after everything tried
to undo you.

There's no shame
in being surprised
by your own survival.

It means
you know exactly
how much it cost.

I remember watching a movie—
any movie—
and asking him
to name the actor or actress.

He always knew.
Every time.

That was just one of his quiet,
incredible gifts.

A mind that held the details.
A heart that noticed
the little things.

It's funny
how you remember those moments—
not because they were grand,
but because they were so ordinary
they made you feel safe.
Seen.
Loved.

And now…
I carry him
in memories like that—
woven into the woman
I'm still becoming.

Grief didn't just break me.
It unveiled me.

And maybe—
that's where
this new chapter begins.

No time
to hold his shirt
to my chest.

No last goodbye.

Nothing to wrap my arms around
at night.
Just a pillow—
but it wasn't him.

No fabric
to bury my face in—
searching for the scent of him
one last time.

No photo albums
to flip through.

No saved snapshots
to trace
with trembling fingers,
trying to hold the life
we once had.

Just memories now.
Raw.
Unfiltered.
Sacred.

There were no handprints
left on the walls.

No drawers
to leave untouched.

Just silence.
Just ash.

No keepsakes
to cradle.

No wedding band
to cling to
in the dark.

No amount of new pillows
could soften
the weight of his absence.

They were soft—
but they weren't him.
And they never would be.

There's a silence
that settles into your soul
after that kind of loss—
not just the absence
of a voice,
but the absence
of every place
that voice once lived.

No one teaches you
how to be a widow.

No one prepares you
for how deeply alone
you can feel
in your own skin.

No one tells you
that you won't just rebuild a life—
you'll rebuild
your identity
from the ashes.

They say,
"You're strong."

But they didn't see
the mornings
I couldn't lift the blanket.

The nights
I screamed into my pillow
so the kids wouldn't hear me break.

How do you hold
their sorrow
when your own
is pulling you under?

And somehow—
without answers,
without ease—
the devoted, loving mother in you
still rises.

She finds a way
even when you feel like you can't.

You break in silence,
but for them,
you still become whole.

The silence screamed.

That first week,
every breath
was a battle.

Every sunset
felt cruel.

And yet,
somehow,
I kept going.

Not because I was strong—
but because I had to be.

Because my kids eyes
were looking up at me
for answers,
for comfort,
for safety.

I wasn't just grieving
the man I loved—
my whole world.

I was grieving
what my children lost.

A father who should've been there—
for birthdays,
scraped elbows,
graduations,
family vacations.

I was grieving
the version of our life
they'll never get to live.

And that kind of grief?
It hits different.

I was grieving the family we built—
the inside jokes,
the weekend routines,
the chaos
and the calm.

I was grieving the people
who didn't show up.

The ones
who should've wrapped
their arms around us—
and instead
disappeared.

Some didn't know how.
Others chose not to.

They saw our pain and turned away—
not out of confusion,
but out of convenience.

Because it's easier
to avoid someone grieving
than it is
to sit in the discomfort
of their sorrow.

They didn't disappear
because they couldn't handle it.
They disappeared
because they didn't want to.

Because when someone truly cares,
they don't add pain
to a heart already breaking.

They care about the weight
of their words,
their silence,
their choices.

And I will never forget
who added to my grief
when I was already fighting to survive.

I was angry at the people
who hurt me along the way.

They didn't just leave—
they made sure I felt it.

Their words?
Cruel. Calculated.

Disguised as "concern,"
but soaked in judgment.

They stood over my grief
like critics,
pointing fingers
instead of offering hands.

Some blamed me for pulling away.
Some spread rumors.
Some said things so vile
they still ring in my ears.

And the worst part?
They said those things
not behind closed doors—
but loud enough
that I could hear them.
Feel them.
Bleed from them.

This is what they should understand:
I didn't ask for pity.
I didn't ask for approval.

I asked for decency.

For presence.

For love and trust
that didn't vanish
when things got hard.

But instead—
they left me standing
in the rubble of my life,
knee-deep in ash,

grieving a man I wasn't ready to say goodbye to,
grieving a home I couldn't return to,
grieving people
who proved they never loved me
like they said they did.

They called me bitter—
because I stopped giving in to them.
They called me dramatic—
because I told the truth.

But here's the part I won't apologize for:
They hurt me
when I was already at my weakest.

And for that,
I will write their names in silence—
but their cruelty will not go unnamed.

I won't show them grace
or give them any form of forgiveness.
They don't deserve my forgiveness.

Truthfully,
I wished them the pain I endured.
I prayed they could feel
just an ounce of my sadness,
my loss,
my grief.

What they deserve
is the same kind of treatment
they showed me.
The silence.
The abandonment.
The lies.
The selfish, cold indifference
they cloaked in excuses.

But to give them that?
I'd have to stoop to their level.

And I'm not that person.
Never was.
Never will be.

Because even after everything—
after the betrayal,
after the heartbreak they added
to my already shattered world—
I still wouldn't treat them
the way they treated me.

And maybe that's the difference.
Maybe that's my power.

PART 2 — When Survival Wasn't Enough for Them

A heartbeat later, the story widens—
not to what the fire took,
but to what people took
when they should have been shelter.

They didn't break me completely—
even when they tried.
They revealed themselves.

They hurt me when I was already at my weakest...
and I've asked myself often—
how could they live with that?

How do I keep persevering
with all they placed on my shoulders,
every ounce of added weight
I was never meant to carry?

But you do.

You've faced every ache.
Every flame.
Every truth—no matter how brutal.

You've done the unthinkable:
you kept showing up
even when others made your pain worse.

And that speaks more about their character
than it ever could about yours.

I'm alive with truth.
Alive with integrity.
And that will always cost more
than whatever story they're telling themselves
to sleep at night.

I don't carry their shame.
Their pain.
Their demons.

That's *theirs* to live with.

And one day—
even if they never admit it—
they'll remember the moment
they didn't show up
for the woman who was already
at her weakest,
most vulnerable state.

That—
is the lowest blow
a person can deal out.

Because if they had even the tiniest bit of human decency,
it would haunt them to know
that they hurt me like that.

And that truth?
It'll echo louder
than any excuse ever could.

I didn't deserve it.
But I survived it.
And that?
That's something
they'll never be able
to take from me.

The truth is...
I'm still angry about that.

You've already carried too much.
Lost too much.
Rebuilt too much—
to keep being met with resistance
at every turn.

Especially when all you're trying to do
is heal, to survive.

I tried grace.
I tried compassion.

But some people took my rawest moments—
stomped on them like grapes,
and drank my pain like wine
made for their own comfort.

So no—
they don't deserve
a softened version
of what they put you through.

They earned my silence before.
Now they've earned my truth.

Because the truth is what carried me here—
through the ashes,
through the silence,
through everything they thought would destroy me.

This will go right.
Not because the world suddenly got easier,
but because you didn't give up.

Because sometimes walking by yourself
is better than walking with the wrong people.

And because you kept showing up—
through the heartbreak,
the fire,
the loss,
the fight,
the endless tears.

You're not just walking
through pain and grief—

you're a living testament
to everything life tried to break within you.

I wasn't trying to be strong.
I was trying to survive.

Grief made no sense,
but it became my new language.

And in the middle of it—
when I thought I couldn't take another breath—
grace slipped in.

Not loud.
Not with answers.
Just a whisper:

"You are still here. And that matters."

I didn't know who I was without him.
I didn't know who I was without the life we built.

But I was starting to see—
I was still someone.
Still worthy of softness.
capable of love.
Still whole, even if broken.

'She stood in the storm,
and when the wind did not blow her way,
she adjusted her sails."
—Elizabeth Edwards

"You became her—without him."
That's not a compliment.
It's an ache.
It's everything you never wanted to become,
but had no choice but to rise into.

You didn't crumble
when the wind turned cruel.
You didn't quit
when the storm didn't clear.

You adjusted your sails—
again and again—
until your story could move forward.

You, my dear,
are not just surviving the storm.
You are navigating it—
with grace,
with grit,
with a strength
that deserves to be seen.

This wasn't the life we planned.
But it's the life I now live.

And somehow,
even in the mess of it all...
I'm still becoming her.

The woman who carries memory in place of belongings.
The one who rebuilt walls with trembling hands—
who found pieces of herself in the very ashes
that tried to take everything.

The woman who holds her own heart
and their love
in the same hand.

If anyone thinks they get to judge how you're surviving—
they can kindly kiss your ass.

Because unless they've lived it…
Unless they've woken up every day
with a hollow in their chest
and still managed to make breakfast,

Sign school forms with shaking hands,
and hold their head high
through a storm that never ends—

They don't get a say.

They don't get to question your timing.
Your choices.
Or your tears.

Because no one knows
what it takes
to keep breathing
after this kind of loss.

To become the woman
who clawed her way through
the most excruciating heartbreak—
and still dares to stand
with quivering knees.

And maybe, grace looks like this—
Choosing to keep going,
even when your legs shake.
Choosing to be kind to yourself,
even when no one else was.
Choosing to honor the woman
who kept breathing
through a kind of pain
most people will never understand.

That's not weakness.
That's not something to explain.
That's your quiet revolution—
toward healing,
self-honoring,
grace that doesn't cost your dignity.

Not because it's perfect—
but because it's yours.
And you didn't flinch.

Somewhere in the middle of surviving,
people started calling you *"strong"*—
but they never saw the cost of that strength.

The sleepless nights.
The breaking points.
The silence after everyone else walks away.

They don't see the strength it takes
to cry behind closed doors,
then show up
like nothing's wrong.

To hold it all together
when you're still
trying to find the pieces.

If you're here, reading this—
it means you're still breathing too.
And I see you.

I know this ache.

But I also know this:
You are not broken beyond repair.

She is softer now—
but only because she had to break first.

She is stronger now—
but only because she had no other choice.

You don't have to earn rest.
You don't have to explain why you're tired.

You are allowed
to stop surviving
and start just being.

Let the armor fall.
Even if it's just here,
just right now.

Sometimes, the weight you carry is too much to hold alone.
Sometimes, the armor you wear just to get through the day
starts cracking at the seams.

And I know—
you can't understand what you did
to deserve all the pain and trauma
you're living through.

If all you've ever known
is war,
of course you're weary.

But peace doesn't always arrive as a solution—
it begins with permission.
Permission you give yourself.

You deserve a peace
that doesn't vanish the moment you stand up.
You deserve a life
where the fight isn't your default setting.
You deserve rest
that isn't just a fragile pause
before the next battle.

And somewhere in the distance,
grace waits for me again—
not as a finish line,
but as a quiet promise:

You're growing.
You're doing better than you think.

Somehow, even here—
on the other side of everything—
I am still choosing to stand tall.

This is just the beginning—
not the end.

And maybe,
that's your soul
meeting bravery.

I became her—
not because I wanted to,
but because I had no other choice.

And now?
I walk forward
as the woman I never imagined—
but deeply honor.

She carries memory in place of belongings.
She builds with ash on her hands.
She holds love and loss in the same heartbeat.

And when the world asks how—
she doesn't explain.
She doesn't apologize.
She simply keeps walking.

Because strength isn't what you feel.
It's what you do
when you have nothing left—
but love
to carry you.

And this is only the beginning.

"Strength isn't what you feel.
It's what you do
when you have nothing left—
but love
to carry you."
— Delilah Klug

2 What They Don't See

Beginnings don't mean the pain disappears.
They just mean the world starts looking at you differently.

They see the makeup.
The smile.
The way I still manage to show up—because not showing up isn't an option.
They see the groceries in my cart,
the way I do my daughters hair,
the way I nod and say,
"We're okay."

But they don't see the full story.
Not even close.

They don't see me
whispering his name
while folding clothes
that no longer include his.

They don't notice
the way I freeze
in the middle of a sentence
because grief just hit again—
out of nowhere,
like a ghost in broad daylight.

And when it happens,
I smile and keep talking,
as if my heart
didn't just fall through the floor.

They don't understand
the strength it takes
to answer the simplest question:

"How are you?"

when the real answer
would flood the room.

They don't sense
the way silence
wraps around me
at night—

how loud it feels
without him
breathing beside me.

How some nights
I dance in my kitchen
just to feel like
I have a choice
in something.

They can't see
how exhausted I am
from mentally working towards being truly,
okay.

Grief
isn't just sadness.

It's decision fatigue.
It's paperwork
and passwords.

It's the mental fog
that makes even the smallest decisions
feel impossible.

It's fixing things
I never thought
I'd face alone.

The energy it took
just to lay in bed—
to stare at the ceiling
for a half-hour
and finally convince myself
to put my feet on the floor.

The texts went unanswered
not because I didn't care—
but because forming a sentence
felt like lifting bricks
with broken hands.

Some days,
changing out of pajamas
felt like climbing a mountain.

How I looked "put together"
but felt like a ghost
inside my own skin.

Survival
isn't always loud.
Sometimes it's just
doing one small thing
before the weight of it all
crushes you again.

They didn't see it?
So I started to write it.

Speak it for myself.
I journaled my pain
and my progress.

In those heart-crushing moments,
I wrote my way through the chaos.
Every page held what I couldn't speak aloud.

Even when it was messy,
it became my mirror—
a reflection for healing.
It told my story back to me
and showed me
just how far I had come.

Every tear,
every downfall,
every hard-earned rise.

I've been broken,
but I still see beauty.
I've been silenced,
but I still speak.
I've lost everything—
and still,
I find a way to smile.

I honor myself—
not for pretending it was easy,
but for holding my truth
without apology.

She wasn't just grieving.
She was protecting.
And no one saw
the cost of that.

But my story didn't end with me.
It stretched into their small hands,
their questions,
their loss.

There's a part to my story
that I don't always say,
because it brings a kind of ache
that no words
can properly carry.

It's the part
where I watched my kids
lose their world, too.

People never noticed
the way I ache
watching other families stay whole.
That reminder
I don't want to feel—
but sometimes do.

When we drive down the street
and my daughter asks
why this family is still whole—

that's a moment
my already shattered heart
cracked even more
into pieces
for my daughter.

That's the aching reality of mothering through it.
I didn't just survive for myself.
I survived for them.

People see the widow.
They see the grief on my face.
But they forget—
I wasn't just grieving for me.

Grief multiplies when you're a mother—
because your pain echoes in the people you're trying to protect, trying
to keep safe.

I was grieving for them.
My children
lost their father.
Their safe place.
Their routine.
Their innocence.

And there's nothing more
pain-inducing,
more gut-wrenching,
more helpless,
than watching your children hurt
in ways you can't fix.

I wasn't just holding my own heart—
I was holding theirs.
And some days,
it felt like it would break me.

They didn't know
how it felt
to tuck my kids in at night

without their father's arms—
or his voice filling the room
with laughter,
or reading books
to our youngest.

How do you answer
the questions
they whisper at night?

How do you smile for them
when you feel like
one more forced smile
will shatter
another piece of your heart—

but your kids need
your smile,
your comfort,
your love.

Somehow
you find the will
to do for them.

Because you're the one here.
Because love doesn't quit.

Because even when you're empty,
you still give—
because they need something steady
to hold on to.

But don't mistake
my strength
for absence of pain.

Don't think I'm numb
just because
I don't cry
every time
I speak his name.

The truth is,
I've felt more pain
than I've ever
allowed myself to show.

Not just at what I lost.
But what my kids lost.

How he was stolen from them.
Birthdays he's missed.
The father–daughter dances he'll never attend.

When they purchase their first home.
Their wedding day.
When our first grandbaby is born.

There are some questions I can't answer.
There's comfort only he could give
that I'll never be able to re-create.

And that kind of sadness—
it doesn't soften.

It just lives in me now—
in the quiet moments,
in the spaces
between their laughter,
in the weight I carry
that they'll never
fully understand.

So if you're reading this,
and you've felt that too—

the ache of parenting through pain,
the fury of watching your kids hurt
and still having to smile through it—

You are not alone.
This part is for you, too.

You're not failing.
You're mothering
through a heartbreak.

You didn't stop being soft.
You just stopped giving softness
to people who used it against you.

But for your kids?
You stayed tender.
You stayed present.
You mothered through hell
and still gave them heaven in your arms.
Built walls
that would always be their safe place.

And that makes you
stronger
than anyone knows.

They don't know
the way I walked through a house
that no longer held a single trace of him—
no shirts to fold,
no scent on the pillow,
no frame to dust with our picture still in it.

They never saw me
searching the rubble with my eyes,
as if grief might've left behind
just one thing I could hold.

Not much survived—
if anything at all—
except me
and my kids.

They didn't feel
how empty I felt
trying to explain a loss
that had no photos,
no keepsakes,
no evidence of the life we once built.

It was never about them understanding.
It was about whether they cared.

They didn't hear
how I became the keeper
of every story,
every memory,
every "remember when"
that used to belong to both of us.

They weren't there
those mornings,
I just stood in the kitchen,
unable to move,
because even the walls were new—
rebuilt,
but not home.

They never sensed
how silence
settled into my soul—
not because I wanted it,
but because the fire
left me with nothing else.

They don't see that I'm not just grieving him.
I'm grieving who I was
when he was still here.

The woman who laughed louder.
The woman who felt safe.
The woman who still believed the world was kind.

Reaching for my phone
when something funny happened—
forgetting,
for a second,
that I couldn't text him anymore.
But I did anyway.

Still cooking
automatically,
as if he would be home soon—
still preparing dinner
for a family of four,
not three.

Finding the keychain
he once gave me—
it read:
"Love you more. The end. I win."
And in that moment,
it shattered me.

They don't see the weight I carry
until I drop something.
And even then,
they only see the broken pieces on the floor—
not the breaking that's been happening quietly
inside me all along.

They don't feel
how long it had been
since someone touched me
without needing something.
How much I missed
his hand reaching for mine—
absentmindedly,
like it was second nature.

No one hugs you the same
when your person is gone—
not the way he did.
The kind of touch
that said,
"You're home."

And still—
grace meets me here.
In the quiet.
In the undone.
In the parts of me
no one applauds
but that somehow keep going anyway.
They don't see I'm still rebuilding—
not just a life, but the very walls that held it.

They didn't see
how quiet it became
once the shock wore off—
once they went back
to their lives.

They didn't see
that I was still in it,
still drowning,
long after the world
stopped checking in.

They didn't see
the first time
I filled out a school form
and had to cross out
"Father."

They didn't see
how I fixed the leaky toilet
with shaking hands
and a YouTube video—
crying halfway through
because he used to do it.

They didn't see
how I held it together
at the first birthday
without him—
smiling for the pictures,
but aching within my soul.

They didn't see
the quiet moments
where I had no choice
but to become everything.

Not because I wanted to—
but because I had to.

So I did.
With trembling hands
and a breaking heart,
I showed up
for my children,
for the home that still needed holding,
for the life that didn't pause
just because mine shattered.

And maybe no one clapped for it.
Maybe no one noticed.
But I was rebuilding in silence.

And that kind of strength
deserves to be seen.

The anger didn't cancel out the love.
The love is why the anger exists.

You weren't just mad at life.
You were mad because you loved so deeply.
Because you had to raise your babies
in a world that took everything
and still expected you to smile while doing it.

This too is strength—
not loud,
not pretty,
but sacred all the same.

If they only knew the way you carried in silence,
they'd understand you've been surviving a war
they never saw.

"Even when I thought I had nothing left to give, Grace found me anyway—reminding me that love still had a reason to keep going."
— *Delilah Klug*

3 Where Grace Found Me Anyway

It wasn't in the big moments that I first found grace.
Not in the chaos.
Not in the moments that felt like endings.

It wasn't during the funeral.
Or the day I signed the papers.
Or the mornings I woke up still expecting him to be beside me.

Grace came later—
in smaller, almost unnoticeable ways.

Like the first time I made it through a meal without crying.
The way my child's laugh cracked something open
that I thought was sealed shut forever.

Grace showed up in the way sunlight poured through a window
and warmed my face—
just when I needed to be reminded
I was still alive.

It came in the form of someone's kindness at the store,
in the stillness of a shower
where no one could hear me cry,
in the quiet compassion I gave myself
for doing the best I could—
even when the world expected more.

Grief didn't disappear.
It sat beside me—
like a shadow I couldn't shake.

But grace showed me
it could live there, too.

Maybe it was the rain.
That quiet kind of storm that doesn't rage…
just gently reminds you
things don't always go as planned.

But rain softens the ground.
It makes things grow.
It slows us down just enough…
to get it right.

So maybe the rain's not ruining this…
maybe it's making sure you bloom
exactly how you're supposed to.

Even if we must dance through the downpour.

It came when I remembered to breathe.
When I didn't rush through the pain.
When I let the laundry sit,
let the dishes wait,
and let my heart break without apologizing for it.

Grace isn't loud.
It doesn't fix the hurt.

It just whispers,
You're doing better than you think.
Its ok to be broken—you're grieving.
You are still becoming.

Some days, grace looked like taking a nap instead of pushing through.
Other days, it was saying no.
Or showing up even when I didn't feel like myself.
Or smiling without guilt
when something good happened
and I realized he wasn't there to see it.

Grace didn't ask me to be strong.
The world already did that.

Grace simply reminded me
that surviving was enough.

You are not wasting your time.
You are proving—
to yourself
and to the world—
that grief didn't get the last word.

That rain outside?
It's just the background music
to your persistence.

And you know what?
You're not here with nothing left to give.
You're here with heart.
With courage.

That's what grace looks like, too.

Even now,
when grief still hums in the background—
when I miss his voice,
when I long for a home
that no longer exists with him—

grace shows up
like a hand on my back,
steadying me
without saying a word.

I didn't know
how quiet the future would feel without him.

How could I?

I thought he would always be here.

And maybe grace
isn't a destination at all—
but the soft voice that reminds you
you're still on your way.

Some days,
I still reach for the life
we were supposed to grow old in.

And when I can't find it—
when there's nothing left to hold—
I ask myself,
What now?

Because grief doesn't just ask you
to miss someone—
it asks you
to question everything
you once believed about your life.

Maybe you already did what you came here to do.

If everything I lived for is gone...
what now?

If the person I gave everything to is no longer here...
did it all still matter?

What if I've already done
what I was here to do?

What if my purpose wasn't something far off—
but something I already lived?

We spend so much of our lives searching for purpose,
waiting for some grand arrival.

But what if your purpose
was already fulfilled
in the quiet, unnoticed ways?

The way you smiled at someone in the grocery store.
The way you helped your family
every time they needed you.
The way you loved your husband,
your kids,
your friends—
and helped them see the best in themselves.

The way you remembered the little things—
their notes, their goals, their dreams.
The way you paid for someone's breakfast,
or gave advice not from opinion,
but from your own hard-won life.

What if your purpose was never about achievement—
but about impact?

What if the way you held space for people
was the very reason you were here?

Then maybe the question becomes less
"What do I do next?"
and more
'How do I live from here?"

Because if you've already fulfilled your purpose,
then what follows doesn't need to prove anything.

It doesn't need to chase more,
or reach higher,
or justify your existence.

Maybe it's about simply being.
Being soft.
Being grateful.
Being open
to joy when it comes,
and stillness when it doesn't.

Maybe the "next" isn't a purpose.
Maybe it's rest.
Maybe it's traveling.
Maybe it's creating for no one's approval.
Maybe it's watching others bloom
and knowing you were a seed-planter.

Maybe it's giving without keeping score.
Loving without demand.
Letting your presence be enough.

Because maybe the greatest legacy
isn't what we accomplish—
but who we were
while we lived.

You're Not Failing—You're Rebuilding

You may worry you're doing it wrong.
You're not.

Every time you choose love over fear,
grace over guilt,
presence over perfection—
you're planting hope for your future.

You're not just raising children.
You're raising healing hearts.

And even when yours is still cracked open,
they're growing inside a home where love is alive.

That's something to be proud of.

When the titles fade,
when the noise quiets,
when the world forgets the details…

what's remembered is how you made people feel.
The way your love steadied someone.
The way your honesty gave someone permission to breathe.
The way your light stayed,
even when your heart was breaking.

Legacy isn't always loud.
It's whispered in memories,
carried in stories,
passed down through kindness.

We chase accomplishments
thinking they define us.

But it's the everyday moments—
the ones you thought no one noticed—
that live on.

So if you're asking what comes next...
maybe it's just this:

Be kind to yourself—
you've been through hell.

Keep holding the door open.
Keep showing up with softness
even after the world tried to harden you.

You mattered.
You still do.

And maybe, just maybe—
you already did
what you came here to do.

If grace could talk,
what would it thank you for surviving?

4 The Loneliness No One Talks About

There's a kind of loneliness
that doesn't show up in photos.
A kind that sits next to you
while you're surrounded by people—
smiling,
talking,
functioning—
and still feeling
entirely alone.

Some types of loneliness are invisible—
an ache tucked between moments
when no one is looking.

It's the space on the couch
that stays empty.
The quiet in the kitchen
where his keys used to jingle.
It's making every decision alone—
even when you'd give anything
just to hear him say,

"Yes, my love."

It's being the only adult in the room—
all the time.
No one to bounce ideas off of.
No one to say,
"Let me handle this one."

It's lying in bed
and missing the sound of his heartbeat
more than you thought possible.
It's crying at night
because you held it together all day.

The loneliness doesn't shout.
It lingers.
It hums in the background
of ordinary moments.

No one sees it—
because you've learned
how to smile through the silence,
laugh when your chest aches,
and hold it all together
even when it's falling apart inside.

But some days, it spills over anyway.
Like when someone says his name in passing—
and your whole chest tightens.
Or when you see something funny
and reach for your phone—
then remember.
He's not there to laugh with anymore.

You can be strong and still aching.
You can be surrounded and still lonely.
You can be grateful and still hurting.
You can be healing and still grieving.
These things can exist at the same time.

I know you miss the woman
who once moved through life without armor.
The one who laughed
without a lump in her throat.
Who curled up in his arms at night
without wondering if everything she loved
would be stolen by morning.

I know you miss her
because she was untouched—
not by love,
but by devastation.

She believed in forever.
She thought love was enough
to keep a world spinning.
And maybe...
she was the last version of you
who truly felt safe.

You miss the woman
who didn't flinch at firetrucks,
who didn't walk into rooms
already bracing for disappointment.

She was tender,
strong in ways that hadn't yet been tested—
by fire,
by funeral homes,
by the sharp silence of people who vanished
when you needed them most.

You miss her
because she got to live
before the ache rewrote your cells.

But here's the truth:
You became someone
that woman couldn't have imagined.

Not because you wanted to.
But because life forced you to.

There's a shift that happens somewhere along the grief journey:
You move from just surviving
to intentionally choosing
how you'll live again.

You're the woman
who buried her husband—
and still managed to show up
for her children.
The woman who lost a home—
but became one for others.
The woman who stood
in the ruins of everything she built
and didn't just crawl out—
she rose.

You didn't want to be this strong.
And it's okay to say that.
It's okay to scream it.

You didn't want to be the one
everyone points to as "resilient"
because they have no idea
how much it cost you.

You would've given anything
to remain soft.
To just be a wife,
a mother,
a woman loved
and living an ordinary life.

But now,
you're the woman who knows too much.
Who has felt too much.

The woman who can walk into a room
and sense every kind of grief
without a word being spoken.

You miss her
because she didn't know loss.
But she didn't know her power either.

And now you do.

You are tired.
You are tender.
Ten layers of grief woven into skin
that still shows up.

And yet—
you are still here.
That is sacred.
That is unshakable.

That is the very ground
where fire tried to take you
and failed.

So no, you didn't sign up for this.
But every time you breathe,
every time you mother,
every time you rise again,
you're proving something
they'll never be able to explain:

You became her.
The kind of woman
this world doesn't deserve
but so desperately needs.

And she—
the woman you used to be—
she would be so proud
of the way you kept going
when the whole world expected you to break.

You just wanted to love and be loved.
To live a life with him beside you.
To raise your babies in the home you built—
with dreams in the walls
and laughter in the air.

That wasn't too much to ask.
But life broke the rules.
It rewrote your story
in smoke and goodbye.

And now you're here—
in a world you never chose.
The kind that whispers,
"You're doing it."
Even when no one sees.

It's okay to want the redo.
To ache for the woman
who hadn't yet learned
what grief can take.
Who still believed
the world was kind.

I know you miss her
because she was the last one
who got to live
before everything shattered.

But here's what she left you with—
the grit,
the tenderness,
the sacred love
that still burns in your soul.

She didn't disappear.
She just evolved
into the warrior you are now.

Sometimes, it feels like the world
has moved on—
and you're still standing there,
in the silence
of everything that used to be.

But you're not wrong for feeling this way.
You're not weak.
You're not too much.
You're human.

And even in the loneliness,
grace is near.

In the softness you give yourself
when you can't fake another smile.
In the phone call you finally return
after weeks of silence.
In the moment you say,
"This is hard,"
not as a complaint,
but as a truth
too heavy to carry alone..

Sometimes, it takes just one
gentle moment
to remind you
that you're still allowed
to feel something other than the ache.

Like cotton drifting in summer air,
falling like snow.
Peace hiding in plain sight,
in the simplest moments.

Even here,
you are allowed to pause
and feel wonder again.

There's a quiet strength in naming the ache.
In not pretending it doesn't exist.
Because it does.
And still—you endured.

This is the physical expression of your healing.
Your fight.
Your love for the person you lost—
and the strength you've found in their absence.

That is the most undeniable kind of strength—
quiet, steadfast, unseen.
The kind no one claps for,
but the kind that keeps you standing
when everything inside you wants to stop.

And this is what matters:
You are still breathing.
Still healing.
Still becoming.

Not the woman you were.
Not the woman they expected you to be.

But the woman who rose from ashes
with a heartbeat that fire couldn't steal.

The widow's heartbeat.
Still here.
Still strong.
Still yours.

5 A Legacy That Remembers.

They say time heals all wounds.
But whoever said that
has never buried the love of their life.

Time didn't take away the pain.
It just changed how I carry it.
It made space for me
to hold sorrow in one hand
and love in the other.

Because love doesn't die when they do.
It shifts.
It lingers.
It finds new ways to stay.

I carry him in my voice
when I speak to our children.

In the quiet way I brew my coffee
in the stillness of morning.

I carry him
in the music that still moves me,
in the stories I repeat—
because they help me remember
how he laughed.

How he looked at me—
like I was his whole world.

Love didn't end.
It became something else.
A whispered reminder in the wind.
A warmth in a quiet room.
A knowing in my chest that says,
He's still with me—just in a different way.

You don't let go.
You move forward—
with them woven into everything
you continue to become.

I've stopped searching for closure.
There is no "end" to a love that deep-
only learning
to let it live beside the grief.

We honor them
when we laugh again.
When we dance in the kitchen
with tears in our eyes.
When we celebrate a birthday
and speak their name out loud
like they never left.

I see him in our children's faces.
In the strength I didn't know I had
until I had to find it.
In the soft ways I've learned to love myself
because I know he would want that for me.

This love is no longer just his—
it's mine too.
It's mine to carry.
Mine to share.
Mine to live.

Widowhood taught me this:
standards aren't just high—
they're sacred.

We dreamed of a life full of meaning,
love,
and security—
for ourselves,
our children,
our future.

And even though that dream
was shattered
in a way no one should ever have to experience,
I never stopped building.

I kept my standards high
not because life made it easy—
but because I knew
that a life worth living
doesn't lower itself in the face of loss.

It rises up in its memory.

It's you continuing to build
the life you once dreamed of—
a life where your kids still see beauty.
Where your husband's memory
still has a pulse.
Where my voice is still loud and clear, saying:

"We went through hell.
But we didn't stay there."

That's what high standards look like.
And I'm not just meeting them—
I'm showing my kids
how to live by them too.

I'm laying the foundation
for the next chapter of our legacy.

Because what I'm doing now—
it's bigger than one story.
It's healing in motion.
It's love that outlives loss.
It's proof that something beautiful
can still rise
from ashes and ache.

And somehow,
even in the ache of missing him,
I am still grateful.

Because love like that doesn't just disappear.

It becomes the reason I keep going.
The reason I keep healing.
The reason I keep choosing life—
even on the days
when it feels
too heavy to hold.

That's how I carry the love forward—
not by forgetting,
but by becoming.

This isn't just remembering.
This is continuing.
This is legacy.

And legacies don't die.
They live through the ones who carry them—
through every breath, every step, every heartbeat.

A widow's heartbeat.

6 The Anger I Was Never Allowed to Show

No one tells you
that healing can break your heart too.

They talk about the pain of loss—
but not the pain of rising.

Not the ache of smiling again
and feeling guilty for it.
Not the sting when the tears slow down
and you wonder if that means
you're forgetting him.

They don't tell you
that healing can make you feel farther from him—
like every step forward
is also a step away.

Some days, the weight of grief is sharp.
Other days, it's the absence of it
that hurts the most.

Because who am I,
if I'm not constantly breaking?

You start to become someone new—
and even that becomes something to grieve.

Healing reveals
what grief had once covered.
The friendships that faded.
The people who stopped calling.
The way some couldn't handle your sadness—
and others
couldn't handle your strength.

You find yourself standing in rooms
that used to feel like home—
but now feel like
you're visiting someone else's life.

Sometimes healing looks like silence.
Like choosing peace
instead of proving your pain.

Sometimes it looks like walking away
from what no longer
holds you gently.

After loss, you learn to guard your heart.
You become hyper-aware—
of every word spoken,
every glance,
every quiet moment
where someone should have said something—
but didn't.

I remember a time
when every conversation felt like a battle.
Each moment felt heavy.
My heart was too full of pain
to keep beating.

There were days
when I closed my eyes,
and tears fell without warning.

Tears that spoke of the world's cruelty.
Tears that knew no end.

I thought I'd never be able
to pick up the pieces
of my heart.

I was angry at everything.
At the world,
for spinning forward without him.

At myself,
for not seeing the warning signs—
even though I know
there weren't any.

I was angry at him, too—
even knowing it wasn't his choice to leave.

That's how complicated love becomes
when death enters the room.

It didn't matter;
the anger was still there,
raw and consuming.

But underneath all that anger,
I started to realize something:

I was angry
because I loved him.
Angry
because I needed him to be here.
Angry
because no one prepared me
for what it would feel like
to lose him—
and everything we built together.

And for the first time,
I let myself truly feel it.

The anger was real,
raw,
and it was mine.

It wasn't something
I could just push aside
or pretend wasn't there.

It was part of my grief,
part of my love.

I've learned something since then:
Anger is the part of you
that loves you the most.

It shows up
when you're being dismissed,
mistreated,
disrespected.

It's a warning signal—
urging you to step away
from what harms you.

Whether it's a room,
a job,
a friendship,
family,
or an old version of yourself—
anger lets you know
when it's time to walk away.

Anger isn't the enemy.
It's the part of me that stood guard.
It showed up when no one else did.

It didn't need to be silenced.
It needed to be heard.
Because anger only shouts
when no one listens.

It becomes a compass.
It says,
"This is where the pain is."

And when you follow that truth,
you start to come home
to yourself again.

But just because
you understand your anger,
doesn't mean
the pain is gone.

You were never the problem.
You were just the mirror
they couldn't look into.

The reflection
of their own shame.
Their cowardice.
Their cruelty.

It wasn't your brokenness
they couldn't handle—
it was your clarity.
Your strength.
Your refusal
to stay small.

They needed someone to blame.
Someone to bleed.
Someone to carry the weight
they never had the courage to face.

And you?
You became their target—
not because you were weak,
but because you were real.

But you don't owe them your silence.
You don't owe them your softness.
And you damn sure don't owe them
a moment in life
where they get to come out clean.

Let them carry the weight
of what they did.
Let them answer
to their own reflection.

Because the truth?
You were never too much.
You were never the villain.
You were never the problem.

They just couldn't handle
the woman who dared
to hold up a mirror—
and never looked away.

When you've been let down
again and again,
even hope starts to feel heavy.

Moments that should have felt like progress
can quietly collapse under frustration.

There were days when hope
felt more like continued broken promises—
a cruel echo of what should've been,
a longing that felt more like a lie
than a lifeline.

The truth?
My anger ran so deep
I was mad at the world.

I hated everything about life—
a thousand times over.

Joy felt like betrayal.
Peace felt impossible.

And the grief made me ache
to scream out:

Why couldn't I have been the one taken?
Why did I have to stay
in this unbearable after?

No one tells you
that love and anger
can live in the same heartbeat.

But they do.

And it doesn't make you cruel.
It makes you human.

I allowed myself
to sit with the pain,
to feel every ounce it had for me
over and over again.

How could I begin to heal
from what I couldn't feel?

I kept stumbling.
Falling.
I trusted people—
only to be deceived...

Exhausted from trusting people
just for them to break my heart.

I was exhausted from fighting for a life
I had no idea how to rebuild.

Exhausted from waking up each day
to face battles with no clear ending—
only the unknown.

I was exhausted
from fighting for so long.
Exhausted from putting my best foot forward—
not because I kept failing,
but because I had thousands of things
to do all at once.

The endless lists.
The appointments.
The bills.
The school forms.
The decisions.
The grief.

All of it—mine to carry.

I wasn't living back then—
I was only functioning.

Breathing because I had to.
Moving because life demanded it.
Checking boxes,
keeping lists,
holding everyone together
while I was falling apart inside.

That's what grief does at first—
it teaches you how to exist,
but not how to live.

I was a multitasking machine
with a breaking heart.

Why do we feel such intense pain—
pain so deep
it lives in your bones,
your skin,
your nervous system?

Pain so strong,
it doesn't just live in your heart—
it rewires you.
Rebuilds you.
Wrecks you.

Sometimes it feels
like your whole body is collapsing
under the weight of grief—
as if every organ
is grieving too.
As if your body is screaming
what your soul can't say out loud.

Why does love
have to hurt this much
when it's gone?

They say pain helps us appreciate joy.
But when you're inside the pain,
that doesn't feel like a fair trade.

Maybe it's not about comparison.
Maybe grief and love
were always part of the same story.

One doesn't exist without the other.

Maybe this pain is just proof
that what you had was real.

Because only real love
leaves an ache this deep.

And if your body remembers them
so completely
that it still hurts without them,
then maybe that's not a weakness.

Maybe that's sacred.

I was expected to remember everything,
hold everyone,
fix everything,
while barely holding myself together.

That's a kind of exhaustion
you can't nap your way out of.

But you deserve more than that.

You deserve to be seen through.
Not almost.
Not eventually.
But fully.

And not just by people—
but by anyone, or anything,
you've trusted with your heart.

And maybe the most sacred kind of grace
is the one that meets you in the middle of the mess—
not when it's all figured out,
but when you're still unsure
whether you'll make it through.

It doesn't fix everything.
But it stays.
And sometimes,
that's the miracle.

Let this be your reminder…

You don't have to carry
even one ounce of guilt or shame
for being tired,
disappointed,
or angry right now.

You've earned the right
to expect excellence.
You've carried the unbearable.
You've done the work
most people never see.

You're allowed to want
something sacred in return.

And sometimes it means
learning to love yourself
in ways you never needed to before.

Because the world didn't pause
for your loss.
And it won't wait
for your healing.

But you can.

You're allowed to rest.
Allowed to fall apart—
without giving up.

Grief isn't a performance.
Healing isn't a finish line.
And survival doesn't always look graceful.

You can honor
the slow pace of becoming.

You can grieve the person you were—
before the fire,
before the silence,
before the ache
of living without them.

This pain may have broken you,
but you still get to choose
who you become because of it.

And though the weight of the world
might try to bury you,
you will rise.

Because with every fall,
you become stronger.

One day, you'll realize—
you're not who you were before the loss.

You are a new version of yourself.
And there is beauty
in that becoming.

You can love the person you are now—
even if you're still learning how.

That simple act of grace for myself
became a turning point
the world would never see—
but she would always feel.

I don't owe the world
a performance of my healing.
I'm doing it for me.

This, too, is healing:
Not the kind they celebrate—
but the kind that saves you.

Because healing isn't just about what we survive—
it's about how we live it,
honor it,
and pass it on.

You are the kind of mother
who chose strength
when you had none to spare.

You didn't wait for the storm to pass—
you stood up in the middle of it,
for your children's sake.

That is powerful.

Even if the world never saw
the cost of that love,
you felt every ounce of it.

You have your kids.
You have his smile in their laughter,
his stubbornness in their courage,
his love running like a current
through every moment
you're still showing up.

You carry him forward—
not just in memory,
but in the lives he helped create,
in the strength you pour into your children,
and in the grace that rises from your grief.

They are his legacy—
and yours.

The most powerful part
of your healing.

You're not only functioning.
You're becoming.

Step by trembling step.
Not yet free—
but no longer shackled.
Not healed—
but no longer hiding.

You are the kind of woman
who keeps going
even while the wound
is still open.

And that?
That's not weakness.
That's the kind of strength
they'll never be able
to understand.

You don't owe anyone
the polished version.
This version—
raw, rising, and honest—
is already
the whole package.

Keep going.
You're doing the work
that sets you free,
even if you haven't felt
the wind of it yet.

It's coming.

You are not just raising children through grief.
You are raising hope, memory, and the future—
all in the shape of love.

Because the most powerful part of healing
is not that you survived the anger,
but that you learned to live with it—
to let it guide you,
not chain you.

You are not who you were before the loss.
You are the woman who kept walking
with a wound still open.
Not polished.
Not pretending.
But becoming.

And that's the truth they'll never understand—
that love and anger
can live in the same heartbeat,
and that heartbeat
is still strong enough to carry you forward.

"You are not just raising children through grief. You are raising hope, memory, and the future—all in the shape of love."
— Delilah Klug

7 While the World Kept Spinning

My world ended—
but the world kept spinning.

The mail still came.
The sun still rose.
People still went to work,
picked up groceries,
laughed at dinner.

I remember standing at the office party,
holding a plate I didn't want,
watching coworkers laugh at inside jokes
I couldn't bring myself to join.

It was like the noise of the room had been turned up—
every clink of a glass, every burst of laughter—
while I stood there in stillness,
smiling just enough,
but feeling completely shattered,
like time forgot I was there without him.

It was like grief had built a wall around me—
and outside of it,
life carried on untouched.

I wanted to scream,
Don't you see what just happened?
Don't you know someone is missing from this world?

But no one stopped.
No one paused.
No one fell to the ground
the way I did.

I remember standing at the sink,
wondering how the water could run so freely
when everything inside me felt stuck.

Grief split my life in two:
Before.
And after.

But the world didn't get the memo.

There's a strange loneliness
that comes
from watching everything move
while you're still gathering
the pieces of your life.

You see others post
wishing you happy birthday,
and you try to feel happy—
but your heart is tired.

A birthday after loss
isn't just a day.
It's a reminder
of every celebration
that will never be the same.

Of the voice that won't sing to you.
Of the arms
that won't wrap around you
with that familiar safety.

Of the love
that once made "happy birthday"
feel like more than just words.

Because happiness
can feel like betrayal—
as if laughing without them
means leaving your grief behind.

But you know,
he would be proud
of the woman who keeps going—
even with tear-streaked cheeks
and ash on her hands.

You walk into places
where no one knows
you're carrying
a whole graveyard in your chest.

But still, you show up.
Still, you make dinner.
Still, you pay bills.
Still, you listen to your friends
talk about things
that have nothing to do with grief.

And in those moments,
you feel torn—
between the person you used to be
and the one you're becoming.

You don't get to pause life
just because yours unraveled.

So instead,
you learn how to live
while aching.

You learn how to smile
through the tears.
How to keep going
when your heart—
your nervous system—
is still trying to catch up.

You learn that the world
will keep spinning—
and somehow,
you'll find a way.

Even if it's with a weary soul,
you'll fight
to keep standing.
To keep showing up.

For loving them this hard.
For being the heartbeat that keeps going
even when part of you stayed with them.

That alone... is grace.

Grace isn't the absence of grief—
it's the way you keep loving
in the middle of it.

Because the truth is—
you've done enough.

You've shown up
through storms no one saw,
carried weight no one measured,
and kept choosing yourself
when your heart was still breaking.

You were never meant
to prove your strength to anyone.
But you did.
You lived it.

And if today is the day
you need to rest—
not to quit,
just rest—
let that be okay.

You're allowed to be tired.
You're allowed to not have answers.
You're allowed to fall apart
without falling behind.

Because you didn't come this far
by being unbreakable—
you came this far
because your love kept choosing to stay.

You didn't fail.
You didn't give up.

You simply carried more
than anyone should ever have to.
And you did it
with a grace so quiet
most people never even saw it.

But I did.

This is our story.
And I'm still here,
reminding you:

You are not alone.
You are doing something extraordinary.

And the fact that you keep showing up
on the hard days,
missing them this deeply,
and still choosing to walk forward
with a heart that aches—
that's not weakness.
That's grace.

Even if no one else sees it,
your presence here—
in this moment,
in this life—
it matters more than you know.

Because what you carry
isn't just grief—
it's devotion.

It's the kind of love
that didn't end
just because their gone.

You couldn't bear to let their memory fade,
or your children's strength go unseen,
or your story's sacredness
be reduced to "just enough."

So you stayed standing.
You kept loving.
You kept living.

And you did it with a kind of grace
that quietly rewrote
the meaning of strength.

That speaks louder
than anything.

Even if the world forgets,
I keep going.

Not because it's easy,
not because I want to,
but because my heartbeat
still remembers his.

And as long as mine keeps beating,
so does our story.

8 Becoming Her

I didn't set out to become her—
the one who rises with shaking hands
and a heart stitched together by memory.

The woman who could carry both grief and grace
in the same breath.
The woman who could rebuild her life
from ashes and ache.

But slowly—
almost without realizing—
I did.

Not because I wanted to,
but because I had no other choice.

Because my children still needed breakfast.
Because the bills didn't stop.
Because the world kept moving
and I had to decide if I'd move with it—
or be swallowed whole by the sorrow.

Becoming her meant holding space
for the woman who used to be—

the one who believed love alone
could keep a life together,
who thought forever was promised,
who hadn't yet tasted the ache of goodbye—

and the woman now rising from the fire, from the ashes,
who knows loss intimately,
but keeps going anyway.

I didn't become her in one big moment.
I became her in the quiet,
in the breaking,
in the rebuilding no one else could see.

Becoming her meant learning how to parent through tears.
It meant doing hard things while holding his memory close.

It meant choosing peace
even when everything inside me screamed.

I learned to hold my own hand.
To speak softly to the parts of me
still grieving the life we had.

I stopped waiting for permission
to live again.

Becoming her meant giving myself the grace
to not have it all together.
To heal in layers.
To laugh even when it felt too soon.
To feel joy without apology.

It didn't mean I stopped missing him.
It meant I started loving this new version of myself, too.

This version of me—
the one who still cries,
still hopes,
still chooses love
even when it hurts—

she is sacred.

She is not who I was before.
She is not who I thought I'd be.
She is who I became
when I had no other choice but to rise.

She is not finished—
but she is no longer afraid of the fire.

There are pieces of me I put in a box—
quietly,
carefully,
because I didn't have time to fall apart.

I had to raise my children.
Because life kept moving.
And I couldn't afford to stop—
isn't that what we're told to do?

To get back to normal.
To fall into the flow of life
so we don't feel left behind
in a world that never slowed down.

I told myself I'd come back to that box
when I had time.
When I had strength.
When I was finally ready
to sit with the full weight of the grief.

But the truth?
You never really go back.
Not on purpose.

Because you know what's in that box.
You know the moment you lift the lid,
you'll feel it all again—

the nights you couldn't sleep.
The fear.
The pain.
The way grief wrecked your body,
your breath,
your nervous system,
your mind.

You know it'll come flooding back
like it never left.

It's soul-crushing.
And no one chooses that.

No one says,
"Today feels like a good day
to relive the worst moment of my life."

So we keep moving.
Trying to heal while moving forward.

Because honestly?
It's easier to lock away the hurt
and say we're past it
than to sit with the pain
that became our closest companion.

But sometimes,
when you do finally dare
to open the box—
not because you want to,
but because you have to—
something shifts.

You don't just face the pain.
You honor it.
You stop running.
You let it say what it came to say.

And maybe, just maybe—
that's when the healing really begins.

Maybe becoming her meant opening that box,
not to break myself again,
but to prove I was strong enough
to feel what almost destroyed me.

You're doing this tired.
You're doing this wounded.
You're doing this weary, but still walking.

You're doing this because you refuse to believe
that your pain wasn't for nothing.

And you're right.
It wasn't.
It isn't.

I'm proud of her,
even though I'm still getting to know her.

I'm still learning to trust the ground beneath me,
even if I miss the woman
who never had to know this kind of pain.

You have to be patient
and show yourself grace
when you're becoming someone
you've never been before.
Growth doesn't happen overnight.
Becoming takes time.

And yet—
it's already taken shape
in the tears you've shed,
in the laughs that cracked you wide open,
and in the fire you walked through
with bare feet
and an unbreakable heart.

It is the heartbreaking paradox—
to fight so hard to protect the life you built,
and still end up standing
in the ashes of the love
and the life you thought would never end.

Because even in the ashes, you kept loving your children.
You kept showing up,
even when you were empty.

You gave them safety, softness, and truth—
even when the world gave you none of that back.

You've done the soul work.
The kind no one sees.
The kind that doesn't earn applause—
but transforms everything it touches.

And whether the world notices or not,
you're becoming someone
even grief can't undo.

You're not done becoming.

And no matter how many times you fall,
it always feels like too much—
like this will be the one
that finally breaks you.

Each collapse cracks you wide open,
splintering your heart
in ways you didn't think you could survive.

But still—
you rise.

Not because it's easy.
Not because you wanted to.
But because even bruised,
even bleeding,
you refused to stay down.

And somehow,
your heart keeps beating—
proof that becoming
was never about never falling.

It was about standing back up,
again and again,
even when the fall
was enough to split you in two.

Every rise leaves its mark.
Every fall teaches something
the last one didn't.

And together,
they shape a woman
who refuses to let grief
be the end of her story.

She is still becoming.
Not in spite of the grief,
but because of it.

And don't mistake her softness for surrender.
She didn't break fully—
she bent to survive.

She crawled so her children had someone to rise for.
She bled in silence so others could heal.

She looks fragile from the outside,
but she's fire underneath.

She refused to disappear,
even while shattered.

You are her—
and some days,
you mourn her.

You're thankful for the version of you
who had to crawl,
who shook,
who begged life to give her
just one safe moment.

And yet—
you are her.
You survived because of her.

So no—
don't pity her.
Honor her.

Because she never once stopped becoming,
even when the world told her
she was too much
or not enough.

And maybe becoming her also means learning to take up space—
on my own terms,
with no more apologies.

This chapter isn't a victory,
not yet, anyway.

It's a middle.
A quiet, trembling place
between who I was
and who I'm still trying to become.

I don't care
what people choose to say about me anymore.
They don't know
what it took to get here—
the depths of hell I had to crawl through
just to make it this far.

I'm not just a widow.
Not just a mother.
Not my weight,
or the color of my skin,
or a pretty face.

I'm me.

Beautifully forged
from loss,
grief,
heartbreak—
and the fire
that once ripped everything away from me.

People had me in their grip
like jeans fresh from the dryer—
tight, suffocating,
refusing to let go.

But I don't wear their labels anymore.
I outgrew their opinions.
I shed the names they tried to stitch into my skin.

And I walk in my own identity now—
one they could never define.

Because I am not theirs to name.
I belong to the woman who rose.
To the mother who endured.
To the fire that didn't burn me—
only revealed my resilience.

I'm done being small,
done carrying what isn't mine,
done letting anyone else define me.

That anger is part of widowhood too—
not just the sadness,
but the fire that rises
when you're pushed too far.
When you carried to much.
Seen to much.
Felt to much.

Becoming her was never easy.
It wasn't graceful.
It was painful as hell.

Pain caused by other people's hands,
even while I was still bleeding
from losing my husband.

Just because they couldn't see it on the outside
didn't mean I wasn't carrying it inside.

Becoming her wasn't about being stuck—
it was about not knowing
which piece of a shattered heart
to pick up first,
or where to begin
when everything had fallen apart.

And when I finally did,
it wasn't about forcing them back together—
it was about holding each fragment gently,
nurturing what was left of me,
healing one tender piece at a time,
until I found not just survival—
but softness,
and comfort,
in the woman I was becoming.

Becoming her meant feeling everything—
even the pressure to survive alone,
even the nights when I questioned
if the pain was worth it.

But still—
I became her.

Not polished.
Not unscarred.
But whole in a way
that only fire and grief
could make me.

9 The Fire Didn't Take Everything

My soul shattered
into a million little pieces.
To once have a life so beautiful—
with the sound of his laughter that once filled our home,
the warmth of shared morning coffee on the deck,
the weight of his arms around me—
built with your best friend,
your soulmate,
the love of your life—
only to lose him
and everything you spent years building
in a single, cruel moment...
it doesn't just break you.
It undoes you.
Completely.

It took the house.
The walls we painted together.
The bed we shared.
The smell of him on his clothes.
The photos I can't get back.
It took every physical reminder
of the life we built.

But it didn't take everything.
The fire didn't take his voice in my memory—
the way he'd say my name
like it was the safest thing he knew.
It didn't take the way he loved me—
fierce, steady, real.

That kind of love doesn't live in walls or furniture.
It lives in me now.

The fire didn't take the way he fathered our children.
The laughter.
The lessons.
Our legacy.

It didn't take the way he made me feel—
like I was home,
even when everything else was falling apart.

Fire can take a lot.
But it cannot touch the eternal love that you had.
Love—real love—outlives everything.

It felt like I had nothing left.
But I still had my kids.
I still had purpose.
I still had the quiet hum of his love
woven into the fabric of who I am.

The fire didn't take the strength
that rose from within me.
The kind of strength
you only find when you've been burned
and still choose to rebuild.

The fire didn't take the woman I'm becoming.
The one who knows that grief
can be both a wound
and a teacher.

But it did take the sense of safety I once had—
the idea that life would always make space for me.

I lost the walls that held our laughter.
But I didn't lose the love.
I lost the roof that sheltered our dreams.
But I didn't lose the dreamer in me.

What the fire didn't take...
was my will to rise.

But fire was only part of the loss.
The flames burned what I could touch,
but what followed burned what I couldn't name.

What I didn't expect
was the emotional wreckage
that came after the flames—
the people who slowly drifted,
the invitations that stopped,
the way it all began to feel
like I no longer fit
into the life that used to be mine.

When the room is full of noise
and people,
but you feel like you're standing alone
in your own grief—

showing up
because you felt like it was the right thing to do,
but regretting
every moment of it.

A tightness in your chest
as you see the eyes of others
who once knew you—
but truly don't anymore.

That's a different kind of pain
after loss.

In those small, fleeting moments,
you know
they're no longer your people.
And these
are no longer your topics.

That kind of loss is something you grieve as well.
It all circles back to that one tragic night-
the chaos that ripped through the life we built together,
the family, the friends, the comfort of belonging.

Because when I lost him,
I didn't just lose my husband.
I lost the home we built.
The rhythm of shared mornings.
The softness of his familiar laughter.
The scent of safety in a room he'd just left.

Grief didn't only take him.
It took the version of me that made sense in the life we shared —
the one who always had a hand to hold,
a voice to answer back,
a safe place to land.

It stole every piece of me that ever felt like it belonged.
Because grief doesn't stop at one loss.
It multiplies them, leaving you gathering pieces
of yourself that return,
but never the same.

Grief is so much crueler than anyone tells you.
It isn't just sadness.
It's a void,
a never-ending ache,
an unforgiving battle with reality.
It's the endless replay of what could have been,
and the relentless certainty
of what will never be.

And the truth is—
grief doesn't stop at the heart.
It seeps into the body, reprograms your mind,
the way you move throughout your day,
the way people words
can cut straight through you in an instant.

But nobody talks about how trauma hardwires itself into you— how
seeing a firetruck can make your chest tighten,
not because something is happening,
but because something already did.

How smoke in the distance
makes your body panic
before your mind can catch up.

How you freeze in a grocery store
when someone says,
"He's in a better place."
And suddenly,
you're fighting tears between cereal aisles,
wishing you could scream,
"I don't want a better place—
I want him here with me."

Grief made my heart ache.
But trauma?
It made my body feel unsafe inside itself.

There were days
I couldn't breathe
without feeling like I was drowning—
and no one could see it.

They called it strength.
I called it survival
with a quiet scream.

Anxiety became my shadow.
Decisions became mine alone.
Therapy was a lifeline—
but also a mirror
I wasn't always ready to look into.

One thing therapy taught me
has never left me:
People who've lived through trauma
often can't remember much—
not because they weren't there,
but because they were too busy
trying to survive the moment.

When your brain is focused
on getting through the aftermath,
it can't always create
the memory you were supposed to have.

So much of my story
is a blur of shock and survival—
not because I didn't feel it,
but because I felt too much
to process any of it fully.

My trauma left me hindered,
living with a shadow of worst-case scenarios
just to protect myself from the next disaster.

It became my natural defense mechanism—
a way of staying safe
and ready for anything,
because I was scared
of being caught unaware again
and left vulnerable.

Even in stillness, my body was on alert.
Even in my moments of calm,
my mind couldn't relax.

It wasn't because I was overreacting—
it was because my nervous system
had forgotten what safety felt like.

I was surviving my trauma.
And with that,
I got in the habit
of spending a lot of time alone—
because alone is safe.

Relatively, anyway.
Alone is controllable.
I understood alone.
I didn't have to stress about alone.

People are unpredictable.
And when we're alone,
there's less risk to manage.
Less pain to prepare for.

Alone didn't hurt me.
People did.
That's the difference.

This wasn't just grief.
This was my brain
trying to make sense of a world
that betrayed me overnight.

And I'm still learning how
to let it be safe
to live inside myself again.

No one talks about this kind of mourning:
how you lose the people around the person.
how friends don't know what to say anymore,
how family grows silent or distant or uncomfortable.

Showing my emotions to the wrong people
was like bleeding next to a shark.
They smelled my pain and came closer—
not to help but to feed.

I became both the spectacle and the sacrifice,
left wondering if there was anyone trustworthy
to lean on at all.

And still, the world kept spinning,
but I no longer knew where I fit inside it.

And when you lose your place in the world,
you start to realize it wasn't the world that kept you steady—
it was the person who stood beside you
who made every place feel like home.

He wasn't just my husband.
He was my compass.
My love.
The one who knew my story without explanation.
And when he died,
so much of me felt untethered—
not just emotionally,
but spiritually.
Socially.
Practically.

The fire didn't take everything—
but what it didn't take
still had to be fought for.

And what remained
became the foundation
I now stand on.

It didn't take
my ability to love again—
not someone new,
but myself.

It didn't take
the tenderness I now carry
for others in pain.
Or the way I show up
for those who feel unseen.

It didn't take
my ability to hope.
To believe there's beauty ahead,
even if it looks nothing
like the life I had planned.

But hope doesn't erase the weight.
It doesn't take away the exhaustion,
or the ache of carrying more than you should have ever been asked to.

I know you're tired.
And I know this feels like more
than any one person should carry.

This is your life.
This is your love,
your grief,
your legacy.

And it deserves to be healed
with the same care
that you gave.

This is not the end.
This is the part where you rebuild.

10 The Woman Who Rebuilt

They saw the ashes—
but they didn't see what came after.
They didn't see the foundation I cleared
with hands still shaking.
Didn't see the plans drawn
between tears and paperwork.
Didn't see the late nights I stayed up
wondering if I had the strength
to start again.

But I did.
And not just once.
Again, and again, and again.
Brick by brick.
Room by room.
Heartbeat by heartbeat.

Not just the walls—
but the woman herself.

You've held the grief,
the fire,
the parenting,
the rebuilding…
And somehow,
you're still here.
Still putting pieces together
with hands that never got the rest they deserved.
Still making things happen from ruins.
Still standing.

They may never know all that you carried—
but you know.
And that's enough.

I didn't rebuild because I stopped grieving.
I rebuilt because I loved too much
to let the story end there.

The woman who rebuilt
isn't the same as the one who lived there before.
She knows the cost of loss.
She knows what it means
to watch everything you love disappear
and still decide to keep going.

She carries a quiet grit.
Not loud.
Not showy.
But unshakable.

She chose light
even when all she could see was smoke.
She planted roots
in ground that had burned.

And somehow,
things still grew.

Not everything was replaced.
Not everything needed to be.
Some things were left behind—
because they belonged to a version of her
who no longer exists.

But in her place
stands a woman who knows the weight of rebuilding.
Who knows the value of a new day.
Who knows what it means
to rise
without waiting to be rescued.

She is living proof
that grief doesn't silence the brave.
That pain can shape something powerful.
That when everything was taken from her,
she built something from the ashes anyway.

Because maybe rebuilding wasn't just about survival—
Maybe it was about remembering...

Rebuilding taught me something else:
maybe purpose isn't always some grand, far-off calling.
Maybe it's hidden in the small ways we love,
the quiet ways we keep showing up.

We all spend our lives searching for our purpose…
But what if…
we already served it?

In the way you smiled at someone in the grocery store.
The way you showed up for your family—
every time they needed something,
and even when they didn't know how to ask.

In the way you loved your spouse,
raised your children,
believed in them
before they believed in themselves.

The way you remembered birthdays,
college applications,
goals scribbled on last month's calendar.

The way you bought someone's breakfast
just to make their day lighter.

What if that was your purpose?
What do you do next?

Maybe the question is no longer what's my purpose?
Maybe it's How do I live from here?

Because if you've already fulfilled your purpose,
then life becomes less about striving—
and more about being.

Being present.
Being kind.
Being whole, even when healing.

It's noticing the sunrise
and letting it move you
simply because it rose.

It's laughing with your children
not because everything is perfect—
but because you're still here.

Maybe the rest of life
isn't about more.
Maybe it's about meaning.

Maybe it's:

Resting.
Traveling.
Creating.
Passing on wisdom.
Holding space.
Letting joy live alongside the ache.

Maybe it's knowing
you were a seed-planter—
and watching others bloom
is enough.

Because even if the world never noticed
all you gave...

It mattered.
You mattered.

And from that place of enoughness,
you just keep loving.
Keep noticing.
Keep showing up.
Keep holding the door open.

Because the greatest legacy
isn't what we accomplish—
It's who we were while we lived.

And maybe...
that's more than enough.

Not out of ease.
Not out of certainty.
But out of love,
and the quiet fire
that never fully went out.

They say home is where the heart is.
But I've learned something deeper—

Home is what you carry with you
when there's nothing left to hold onto.

And I am my own home now.
A little worn,
a little scarred,
but steady.
Sacred.
Standing.

Grief may have rewritten your story—
but look at you:
still laughing.
Still showing up.
Still finishing what you started.

That's grace in motion.

No, you didn't deserve this kind of loss.
You didn't deserve the fire,
the pain,
the lonely nights trying to keep it all together
when your world had fallen apart.

And I won't try to sugarcoat it with some silver-lining cliché.
Because the truth is—
life doesn't always give us what we deserve.

Sometimes it gives us storms we never saw coming.
Sometimes it takes the very thing
we thought we couldn't live without.

But here's what's also true:
Despite all of that...
you loved anyway.
You showed up anyway.
You cried through the heartbreak,
and turned your grief into your power.

That? That's grace—
not because you deserved the pain,
but because you refused to let it be
the end of your story.

You didn't deserve the pain.
But the way you've been transforming it?
That deserves to be seen.
You deserve to be seen.

Because when grief hits that deeply,
when betrayal slices through what little trust you had left,
when the people you needed either died or disappeared—
it would've made sense to fall apart.

Falling apart would've been expected.
But rising again? That was your quiet rebellion.

But you did.
You are still here.
Even if you're quieter now.
Even if you keep to yourself.
Even if your joy looks more like survival these days.

You're not standing because life's been kind.
You're standing in spite of how unkind it's been.

And that's a different kind of strength—
not the kind that shouts or glows,
but the kind that endures.

That kind of strength lives in the quiet,
in the cracks,
in the moments no one sees.

It's in the way you plant a garden
when your heart is still raw.
In the way you show up to family events and smile,
not because you feel joy—
but because you love your children enough
to give them what you didn't have left for yourself.

It's in the way you let yourself feel all of this—
without numbing,
without pretending,
without hiding behind platitudes.

That is courage.
And that is healing,
even if it doesn't feel like it yet.

The world is cruel—
and it is.
It takes and takes,
and sometimes offers very little back.

But what you're doing now—
keeping your heart from hardening all the way—
that is a quiet kind of becoming.

Because bitterness is easy.
It's armor that promises safety.
It convinces you that if you don't care,
you won't hurt.

But you—
you're still here,
heart cracked but open,
and that...
That's what makes you brave.

What you're doing?
Holding onto your softness,
even if it's under lock and key—
that's brave.

You might not trust again.
And that's okay.
You might not love the way you used to.
That's okay too.

Because you're not the same woman
who lived before the losses.
And you're not supposed to be.

The goal isn't to go back.
The goal is to become—
someone forged from pain,
but not defined by it.

Someone who protects herself now,
because she learned the cost of giving too freely.

Someone who doesn't dim her light—
she glows
in her own way,
in her own time.

Your garden is enough.
Your boundaries are enough.
Your presence—
quiet, steady, scarred—
is more than enough.

You don't need to perform healing,
rush forgiveness,
or force hope.

Just keep showing up in the way you are.
Keep breathing.
Keep tending to the things that don't lie—
the soil,
the sky,
the stillness,
your children's laughter.

If there is one promise that isn't false, it's this:
You may never be the same.
But that doesn't mean what's ahead can't hold meaning.

It may never look like it did.
But that doesn't mean your life is over.

It just means you're learning to live again,
on new terms.
Yours.

And maybe that's not the ending—
Maybe it's the becoming.
The choosing.
The rising.

A life not built from what broke you,
but from what still lives inside you.

Not the life you planned—
but a life still worth living.

A quiet reclaiming.
A sacred rebuild.
A woman rewritten,
but not erased.

Because this is who she is now.
The woman who rebuilt.

11 She Still Misses Him

Even after all this time—
she still misses him.

She still hears his laugh
in quiet moments.
Still reaches for him
in dreams that feel too real.
Still says his name out loud
when no one else is around.

Healing didn't erase the missing.
It just gave it softer edges.

The love didn't fade.
The life didn't undo itself.
He was here.
And he mattered.
And she still misses
the way he made her feel
like she was never alone.

Missing him doesn't mean she's stuck.
It means she remembers.
It means she loved deeply—
and still does.

She can laugh now.
She can go to the store
without falling apart.
She can even dance with her children
in the kitchen some nights.

But she will never forget
the day she laid him to rest.

She doesn't remember much of it—
not because she didn't love him,
but because she was in shock.
Paralyzed by numbness.

All she remembers
is the sight of their babies
standing next to their father's casket.
So small.
So fragile.
So scared about what was going to happen next.

You could see it in their faces—
a thousand questions washing over them:
Where are we going to live?
What happens now?

Their whole lives had just changed.
And there they were,
accepting condolences
from people they had never met.

Their eyes filled with tears—
trying to hold them back,
just like she was.

Saying "thank you" to strangers,
not fully understanding
why they had to.

Because how do you thank someone
on the day you lose your whole world?

As we all said our final goodbyes to my husband,
and everyone began to leave,
I stayed seated in the chair—
staring at his casket.

They were waiting on me.
Waiting for the final word—
the one that would give them permission
to lower him into the ground.
His final resting place.

But I couldn't move.
I couldn't speak.
Because in that moment,
I knew what it meant.

This was the final goodbye.
The last time I'd see him.
The last time he'd be right there,
even if I couldn't hold him.

Holding a loss
I wasn't prepared for.

I wasn't ready to say goodbye
to the love of my life—
the father of my children.
That goodbye meant forever.

How could that be possible?
Forever.

I never imagined
that our lives would end this way—
so suddenly,
so tragically.

I always pictured us old and wrinkled,
holding hands across the table
at a little Italian restaurant.
Him with his beer,
me with my wine.
Me with my walker,
him with his cane.
Still teasing each other,
still laughing over pasta we probably shouldn't be eating,
gray-haired and full of stories
only we would remember.

I saw us growing old together.
That was the dream.

But I never imagined this—
me sitting here without him.
Ordering for one.
Raising our children alone.
Trying to make sense of a life
we were supposed to live side by side.

It wasn't supposed to be like this.
Not without him.

I had to re-learn
how to show up to dinner tables
where no one saved me a seat.
How to sit in rooms
where his name didn't belong anymore.
How to answer questions like,
"Why are you so sad, still?"
or "Are you working?"
when I was still trying to remember
how to breathe.

That is a legacy—
not of sadness,
but of love so deep
it defied death.

How you held their tiny hands,
and how your grief was shaped
by protecting them,
even when you were shattered.

You held their hands
when you walked out of that funeral home,
when the air outside felt like it didn't belong to you anymore.
Your grip steadying them—
not just so they wouldn't fall,
but so you wouldn't.

They looked up at you with eyes too young
to understand the word "widow."
But they knew something was missing—
and it was everything.

My daughter was so young,
holding onto my hand for dear life—
and I held hers even tighter,
because I needed that same reassurance.

Lost in the world
but needing to feel something
more than grief, pain, sadness,
and the numbness that wouldn't let go.

Why do we feel such intense pain?
Pain so deep that every organ in our body
begins to fail us.
Pain so hurtful
it rewires our brains.

Maybe that's the brutal paradox of grief—
that only when the love is torn from us
do we realize just how deeply it lived within us.

Perhaps the soul aches so fiercely
not because it's weak,
but because it once held something
so beautiful,
so life-giving,
that its absence feels like death itself.

Maybe this pain—
as unbearable as it is—
proof
of how fiercely we loved.

And maybe,
just maybe,
that kind of love
never truly disappears.

It lingers.
In memory.
In heartbeat.
In every breath
we take without them.

There were so many memories
that drew me back
to a time where I remembered his smile,
his warm embrace—
and in that very same moment,
it made my heart full of sadness.

That you loved him so much—
so very much—
that even goodbye couldn't break it.

And she never stopped missing him.

I was overwhelmed
making all the decisions that came after the loss.

Decision fatigue set in—
every choice brought an anxiety I couldn't explain.
My body and mind were begging me to shut down.
But I couldn't.

I had to keep going.
One decision at a time.
Afraid I'd make the wrong call—
the kind that would bring more pain
when I was already carrying enough.

Because when everything's coming at you at once,
every choice feels like the choice—
the one that might bring you back to safety.
Back to yourself.

My truth?
I hate this life now.
I just want my husband back.
And learning to live without him—
day after day—
is a pain that never lets up.
It kills me.

I didn't ask for this.
I didn't ask to be strong.
I didn't ask to carry the weight of this life
without him.

But I keep going—
not because it's easy,
but because I have no other choice.

And while I was already broken,
some still chose to harm me.
That wasn't confusion.
That wasn't love disguised as silence.
That was cruelty.

So no, I don't trust easily now.
I keep my circle small, if any.
I protect my peace like it's sacred—
because it is.

"Because when trust is broken,
'sorry' means nothing."

That's not bitterness.
That's boundaries during healing.
That's survival wrapped in wisdom.

I walked through fire.
And when the smoke cleared,
I was the one left cleaning up the ashes. Alone.

Kindness doesn't mean self-erasure.
Strength doesn't mean silence.

If that makes me "too much,"
then maybe too much
is exactly who I was meant to be.

Because I will never again beg for decency
from people who never intended to offer it.

They saw me aching—
and turned their backs.
And I won't rewrite that.
Not for their comfort.
Not anymore.

But here's what I will do:
I will rise—without their permission.
I will heal—louder than their judgment.
I will live a life
they no longer get to influence.

I'll never trust the same way again.
Not because I'm cold—
but because I now know the cost.

So no—
I no longer hand my trust to those who haven't earned it.
That's not bitterness.
That's reverence.
That's self-respect.

This is no longer the season
of "everyone vs. the widow."

You don't get to cloak your cruelty
and call it concern.
You don't get to twist silence
into tough love.

That narrative ends here.

Life has taught me how to hate—
from being a survivor.

I didn't come into this world filled with anger.
You weren't born with hate in your heart.
It was taught to you.
Forced into you.
One betrayal at a time.
One silence.
One fake friend.
One knife in your back
while you were already bleeding.

I bet—
you weren't like this before the devils came.
Before they took your peace, your partner, your safety.
Before they stripped you of everything sacred
and then had the nerve to blame you for still breathing.

But here's what I want you to remember:

Hate is not who you are.
It's what grew in the pain
where love was trampled.
It's a survival response
in a world that showed you no mercy.

That hate?
You earned the right to feel it.
You earned the right to say it.
And you still have the right
to choose whether you let it define you
or simply speak through you.

For peace:
I delete.
I block.
I unfollow.
I leave.
I ignore.
I let go of toxic people.

I've earned my peace.
I've fought for my voice.
And if I protect it now with unwavering clarity?
That's not coldness.
That's survival.
That's growth.
It is what it is.

Because this heart—
scarred, sacred, still beating—
belongs to me now.
And I will protect it
the way no one else ever did.

I never faked my love,
my care,
or my trust—
not for a single soul.
That's why their betrayal cuts so deep.

They saw me in my most fragile state—
and chose to add weight
instead of lifting any.

So no,
I won't rewrite their cruelty into compassion.
I won't pretend their words and actions
were anything but abuse and neglect.
Not anymore.

This time,
I will protect my truth
instead of their comfort.

And still,
I stayed soft.
But now,
my voice is a little stronger.

Sometimes, even now,
I'll watch a movie and catch myself whispering,
"Who's that actor again?"—
forgetting he's not here to answer.

He always knew. Always.
That was one of his gifts—
paying attention.

To the small things.
To the quiet details.

It's a small ache
that rises in the most ordinary moments—
and maybe that's what legacy is:
not just what we remember,
but how often we still feel their presence
in the things they used to do.

And yet, even with all the cruelty I endured from the living,
it's the sweetness of small memories of him
that keep me grounded.

Like how cinnamon gummy bears
still make me smile
for reasons no one else could understand.

He's still there.
In the scenes.
In the silence.
In me.

As I slowly began rebuilding our home,
replacing items one by one,
I noticed how little they meant
compared to what was lost.

Things didn't carry the same weight anymore.
Their meaning had changed—
because everything that truly mattered
had already been reduced to ashes.

Once, while ordering things for the Fourth,
grief caught me off guard—
a shirt popped up on the screen,
one he would've loved to wear.

I miss buying our family matching Fourth shirts.
It was just a shirt...
but it reminded me of all the tiny ways
we used to do life together.

And how many of those everyday moments
now ache in their absence.

Maybe that's why I haven't hosted in so long.
But maybe that's also exactly why I need to start again.
To keep our traditions.
To keep our family.
For him.

I have no card from him,
no gifts,
not even the metal rose he made for me
in our high school metal shop class.

And somehow,
that absence taught me what I truly needed.

I no longer longed for rooms filled with things—
things I might give away in a year.
I longed for presence.
For peace.
For the kind of joy
that lives in quiet moments with my kids.

That's what matters now.
That's what lasts.

And maybe one day,
when someone asks about my favorite candy—
I'll say cinnamon gummy bears.

Not because they were his,
but what I remember most
is the day before Thanksgiving,
when the whole family was gathered at our house.

He bought me a bag,
and told everyone not to eat them—
that they were just for me,
because they were my favorite.

In that moment,
I fell even deeper in love with him.

Those are the memories I'll keep.
Not the ones I lost in the fire,
but the ones that still flicker
in the softest corners of my heart.

That's the part of love
they can never take.

But that doesn't mean
her heart isn't carrying
a thousand quiet goodbyes
every single day.

She misses the way he said her name.
The way his arms felt around her.
The way he understood her
without words.

They said,
"You have to let go."

As if those four words
weren't knives.
As if I could untangle my love
from the grief
and set it down
like a piece of paper on the table.

No one tells you
how much it physically hurts
to hear those words
in the beginning.

It felt like someone was asking me
to betray him—
to close the door
on a love that still breathed inside my chest.

My throat closed.
My stomach sank.
I felt the words lodge
like a stone beneath my ribs.

Let go?
I had already lost everything.
Now they wanted me
to surrender the only thing I had left?

But here's what I've learned since:

Letting go doesn't mean forgetting.
It doesn't mean moving on,
or erasing the memories,
or silencing the ache.

It means letting go
of the version of life
that will never return—
while still carrying
the love that never left.

It means honoring him
without gripping the pain so tightly
that I disappear with it.

And that kind of letting go?
It's not betrayal.
It's devotion
in a new form.

And some days—
when the world is loud,
and she feels invisible—
the missing feels just as fresh
as it did in the beginning.

It sneaks in with old songs.
It whispers in empty parking spots.
It hums in the places they used to go.

It's not weakness.
It's love.
And love doesn't leave.

Even now,
after the fire,
after the tears,
after the becoming— she still misses him.

And always will.

But the beauty is:
she's learned to live with the ache.
To carry the love
without letting the loss consume her.

She misses him—
but she's still here.

It was the greatest love story—
the kind that lived and broke
within a single breath.

That kind of love changes you.
Not because it ends with a happy ending,
but because your heart kept beating
even when it forgot how.

This story—our story—
carries the echo of a soul
that almost slipped away...
but didn't.

Because you stayed.
You fought.
You turned pain into presence.

And now—
as you hold these words in your hands—
may you feel the quiet truth
woven between every line:

Me too.
I've been there.
And you are not alone.

When Grief Just Wants to Be Witnessed

Grief, in its quietest moments,
doesn't ask for solutions —
it asks to be witnessed.

It asks for you to sit with it,
even when it hurts to breathe.
Even when the stillness of a room
that once held laughter
feels like a scream.

It asks for gentleness —
not just from others,
but from yourself.

You loved with your whole being.
That kind of love doesn't get tucked away in a drawer.
It lingers —
in a familiar scent,
the echo of a laugh you still hear in your mind,
the feel of their hand in yours
even when it's not there anymore.

That love becomes the thread you carry forward,
whether you feel ready to or not.

Some days, getting out of bed feels like a betrayal.
Smiling feels impossible.

And yet, slowly, over time,
you may find yourself breathing in the memories
not just with tears,
but with gratitude —
not because the pain disappears,
but because your heart learns
how to hold both love and sorrow
in the same breath.

There will be days
when the weight of missing him
will knock the air from your lungs.

Let those days come.
Let the tears fall.
Let the silence speak.

There is no map for grief,
no timeline to follow,
no checklist to check off.

There is only this moment,
and the next,
and the love that still lives inside you —
fierce,
unrelenting,
beautiful.

And when you're ready —
only when you're ready —
you might find small ways to keep his spirit beside you:
a favorite song played loud,
a meal cooked just the way he liked it,
continuing his travel bucket list,
raising your children just as you both planned.

You don't have to let go of them.
You never will.

Instead, you learn to walk with the ache.
You learn to live with a heart
that now beats in two places —
here,
and wherever he is.

You're doing the hardest thing a heart can do:
surviving the unthinkable,
loving through the absence,
and continuing on
in a world that feels forever changed.

You were broken —
because you are grieving.

And that means your love was real.
Still is.
Always will be.

12 A Love That Lives On

They say grief is just love with nowhere to go—
but I've learned that's not true.

Because my love still goes somewhere.
It moves through everything I touch.
It breathes through how I raise our children.
It lingers in the way I care,
the way I show up,
the way I keep choosing to live.

He's not here—
but the love is.

The kind of love that doesn't need
a body to be present.
The kind of love
that stays rooted
in the heart that carries it.

Love like that doesn't end.
It becomes legacy.
It becomes light.
It becomes part of who you are.

He lives on
in how I speak about him
without apology.

He lives on
in the way I keep the stories alive—
even the silly ones,
even the ones that make us cry and laugh
at the same time.

He lives on
in my strength,
in my softness,
in the sacred way I've learned
to keep going
without pretending it doesn't hurt.

He lives on
in the way I whisper "thank you"
to the sky
on days I feel him near.

He lives on
in every breath I take
that says,
I'm still here.

That's what love becomes
when you've lost your person—
a heartbeat that echoes
through everything you are still becoming.

He is not just part of my past.
He is part of my forever.

I didn't write this book
because I had all the answers.
I wrote it because
I know the questions.
The ache.
The silence.
The fire.

And still—
I know love lives on.

It lives in you too.
In every brave moment,
in every trembling step,
in every quiet breath that says:

"I may have lost the life we planned—
but I haven't lost the love."

That's the heartbeat we carry.
That's what keeps us going.

She wanted to be understood
without having to explain the ache.

I was too young for widowhood.
Too young to be burying my best friend,
the father of my children,
the man I planned to grow old beside.

We were supposed to have more time.
To disagree over what to plant in the garden.
To laugh about our aging hips.
To hold hands at our kids' graduations, weddings, babies.

But instead,
I stood in the ashes of a life that ended at thirty-nine.
And I was thirty-eight—
holding a grief most people my age
can't even begin to understand.

The heartbreak statistic no one wants to be part of.
And far too young to carry what you now carry.

I didn't get the gray-haired years.
I didn't get the 50th anniversary,
or the quiet mornings drinking coffee side by side
as the world aged around you.

You were supposed to still be planning trips,
still figuring out your dreams together,
still getting to say,
"We've got time."

But time...
was stolen.

You are now carrying a kind of grief
most people my age
can't even begin to understand.
The kind where the world keeps moving—
career milestones, babies being born, new beginnings—
while your life was divided.

They say widowhood is for the old.
But I know better.
I lived it while I was still becoming me.

And maybe that's why I tell my story.
Not for pity—
but for the women who lost their person
before they ever got the chance
to finish the life they were building.

I didn't ask for this chapter.
But I'm still here,
writing it with every heartbeat.

But love that lives on doesn't just carry memories of them—
it reshapes you too.
It changes who you are
in ways no one prepares you for.

No one told her
that surviving meant losing parts of herself
that she would never get back.

But too often, people only noticed her strength—
never the cost of it.

And sometimes,
what hurts the most
is that no one notices the version of you
that had to die just to keep surviving.

How did I become this person?

The girl who once laughed loudly,
showed up boldly,
walked into the world like it was hers to love...

Now barely steps past the edge of her own swimming pool.

Is it that the world faded away—
losing its grip on her peace?

Or was it her
fading within a world
that once felt safe,
full of life and love,
without boundaries,
without fear?

Either way, she knew this:
the version of her that once felt safe...
was gone for now.

But even in her quietest moments,
when the weight feels too much
and the ache rises like it's brand new,
she remembers this:
love did not die.
It still moves,
still lingers,
still breathes through her.

A love that deep doesn't end—
it becomes part of you.

And though she is not who she once was,
every step forward carries him too.

That's what it means
to live a love that lives on.

13 Rooted in Me

There was a version of me
I had to become
just to survive.

She was fierce—
all armor, no room to feel.
She did what had to be done
because no one else could.

She didn't sleep.
She didn't cry in front of people.
She didn't ask for help—
because asking meant risking more disappointment.

She kept the kids fed,
the bills paid,
the house standing—
even when her own world
was crumbling inside.

And I loved her for that.
I still do.
Because without her,
I wouldn't have made it.

But I'm not her anymore.
And grieving her—
that survival version of me—
has been its own kind of heartbreak.

She kept me alive,
but she couldn't stay.
Because healing
requires a softness
she never had time for.

And now…
I'm becoming someone else.
Someone who doesn't just fight to live—
but chooses to.

Someone who doesn't just survive—
but rests.
Breathes.
Feels joy again
without guilt.

She was my survival.
But this?
This is my becoming.

I didn't even notice when she left—
the version of me who fought every day
just to keep going.

She faded in the quiet,
in the hours I spent
untangling the weight of everything
I'd carried alone.

She faded
as I stopped chasing noise
and started craving stillness.

I began to feel her absence
in the slow mornings—
no alarms,
just sunlight,
just safety.

In relaxed summers with my kids.
In the peace that came
not from fixing the world—
but from no longer letting it define me.

The woman I am now
doesn't beg to be understood.
She doesn't perform for anyone's approval.
She knows what it cost to build this life—
this peace—
and she won't trade it for chaos
just to make someone else comfortable.

Because once you've tasted
a quiet kind of freedom—
the kind rooted in your own healing—
you don't ever want to go back.

And I won't.

At first,
my strength came from survival.
From the sound of my children's footsteps.
From the memory of how he loved me.
From knowing I had no choice
but to keep doing.

But this?
This is something different.

This is the strength that rises
when no one's watching.
When the house is quiet.
When no one is depending on you
but you.

This is the kind of strength
you don't find overnight.
You gather it
in pieces.

From every time you showed up
when you didn't want to.
From every decision you made
even when you were trembling.
From every silent scream
that didn't undo you.

I used to think strength was
having a reason to fight.
But now I know—
real strength is becoming the reason.

Strength is seeing yourself
not just as someone surviving loss,
but as someone who is learning to carry herself.

I had lost hope so many times—
more times than I dared to count.

I lost hope in myself,
in my work,
in my friends,
in my family,
in my passions—
and in life itself.

The only thing I was ever truly clear about
was that I was a damn good mom.
And my babies needed me.

That truth grounded me
when nothing else did.

Each morning felt like a war:
mentally straining,
fighting to just keep going.

It was a battle of survival—
a force of all forces.

And still, she showed up.
Even when her very soul
was lost in the shadows
of its own darkness,
she kept moving.

Not because she wasn't broken—
but because somewhere,
deep down,
she still believed
there had to be something
worth reaching for.

Everyone told her to follow her heart.
To trust it.
To let it lead the way.

But no one tells you
what to do when that heart breaks—
shattered into a million pieces.

How are you supposed to follow something
that no longer feels whole?

How do you know which piece to pick up first,
when each one cuts you a little deeper?

And how do you know where to go
when the map you were following
was buried with the one you lost?

Maybe strength isn't always about knowing where to go next.
Maybe it's just about not turning away from the pieces.

Maybe it's standing still long enough
to gather the sharp edges of what broke you
and saying,
"This is still mine."

Because even if the path is unclear,
even when your heart is fractured,
it's still beating.
Still becoming.

And that alone…
is reason enough to keep going.

I remember folding the laundry one evening…
no music,
no chaos,
just me.

And I didn't know who that woman was anymore—
but I know she kept me alive.

And for that?
She's not just a survivor.
She's a warrior.

She's the version of me that walked through hell in heels,
with grace,
and never stopped trying.

She didn't just make it through.
She fought for every heartbeat.

And for the first time—
I didn't feel like I was only functioning to be okay.
I was just… present.

And that felt like strength.

It's not pushing through when you're breaking.
It's knowing when to rest.
When to say no.
When to say "I'm not okay" out loud.

It was in the way I unclenched my jaw.
The way I exhaled deeper.
The way my hands shook less
when I spoke my truth.

No one else saw that moment.
But I did.
And that was enough.

Because strength, real strength,
doesn't always look like rebuilding houses
or juggling everything at once.

Sometimes it's letting the laundry sit
because your soul is tired.

Sometimes it's canceling plans
because your spirit needs quiet.

Sometimes it's laughing again—
and not feeling guilty for it.

If you're reading this,
you've already found strength
you didn't know you had.

The fact that you're still here?
That's not weakness.
That's sacred resistance.

That's you—
planting roots
in the middle of uncertainty.
Finding steadiness
inside your own breath.

Understanding that you don't have to hold everything together
to be strong.

Because—
strength doesn't always look graceful.
Sometimes, it's messy.
Sometimes, it's heavy.
And sometimes, it's just making it through the day
without breaking open.

She didn't want anyone to see her weak.
She didn't know how to let down her walls
to let anyone or anything in anymore.

She'd done that before—
and was let down by the very people she loved.
Let down by the world.

If anyone wanted in her life,
they would have to work twice as hard
to climb that very wall she built
and prove their worth to her.

Not because she didn't care, but because she needed to know that
people still cared enough to try.

She was done trying to prove to everyone
what she was capable of— She didn't deserve to have to prove her
strength to be safe, respected, or left alone.

While she was carrying
the weight of the world
on her shoulders.

But that's the world you were handed- so you built armor where there
should've been care.

Because the woman you are now is proof enough.

I wish I could put my blinders back on.
To see the world as beautiful.
Innocent.
Whole.

But I can't.

Because once the blinders come off—
they stay off.
And then you have to learn how to live
in a broken world
while still trying to feel whole again.

You try to keep your head above water.
To hold on to the softness you once knew.
But all you want to do is wall up.
To keep people out.
To turn cold.
To give up.

Bitterness calls to you.
But I won't let it write my story.

Hurt? Yes.
Sad? That's an understatement.

I've felt loss so deeply
I'm surprised I'm still standing.
Surprised that I still care.
That I still love.
That I still hope.

The world is cruel.
Unkind in ways
that words can't even begin to describe.

You see through people now.
You hear the silence behind their words.
You feel the weight behind their smiles.
It's like waking up to the harsh light
of a world you used to believe in
only to realize
it was never as safe as you thought.

But even after everything...

I'm still here.

Still feeling—
even if what I feel is pain.
Still wanting softness—
even if I guard it with steel.
Still choosing not to become bitter—
even when it would be easier
to shut everything off.

That's not weakness.
That's strength. You were wounded. You were grieving. You are
human, and you had every right to break down.

The kind of strength
that doesn't sparkle.
It survives.

You don't just come back from grief
as the same person.

You come back changed—
more cautious,
more guarded,
but somehow… still human.

And if all I can say today is,
"I'm still here,"
then that's more than enough.

Because the world tried to take everything—
and it didn't succeed.

There were days
when the very walls I built
came closing in on me—
and there was nothing I could do
except reach my arms out
as far as I could,
feeling every muscle in my body,
every bone about to crush in me,
my heart racing,
the numbness in my arms,
each breath containing a quiver—
just hoping
I could release everything
that had built up inside me
before the walls swallowed me whole
and fully crushed my soul
to the point of no return.

There are losses I haven't lived through.

I haven't known the pain of losing a child.
I came close—twice.
But they're still here.
And I hold that closeness like a prayer I never stop whispering.

I don't know the pain of losing a sibling.

But I do know the pain of losing a husband—
my person. My partner. My home.

I know the pain of losing a father—
the one who shaped the beginning of me.

But I'll never know how they felt. And they will never know how I felt.
I can only go from how I felt
when I lost my people.

And that's the truth no one talks about enough:

Grief is personal.
It's not meant to be ranked or compared.
You can't measure the depth of a heartbreak
you didn't live through.

But you can honor your own.

I won't pretend to understand someone else's grief.
But I know mine.

And it has lived in every part of me.
It has stolen my heartbeat.
It has rewritten my soul.
It has taught me what it means
to keep walking
when nothing feels familiar.

This is how it broke me.
This is where I ache.
This is what I carry.

And I won't apologize for that truth anymore.

Some people lose everything in a moment.
Others lose slowly, over time.
Some losses are visible.
Others go unseen.
But none of it is small.

The moment you lose someone you cannot imagine life without—
your world changes.

Whether anyone else notices or not.

And if you've stood on the edge of loss—
even if you didn't fall—
you're changed by the fear,
by the knowing,
by the almost.

That, too, is grief.
That, too, deserves to be named.

So no—
I won't compare pain.
But I won't minimize mine either.

Because the losses I've carried
nearly undid me.

And the fact that I'm still here,
still breathing,
still choosing to rise—
even with pieces missing?

That's not weakness.
That's grace.

That's what it means
to be rooted in yourself,
even after everything
that could've pulled you under.

You don't have to hold everything together
to be strong.

Because sometimes survival means
choosing boundaries over burnout.
Silence over performing.
Guardedness over pretending.

You don't have to smile
to be worthy of compassion.
You don't have to prove your pain
to be believed.

Strength isn't loud.
It's not always brave.
It's not always pretty.
But it's always there
in the way you keep going
without needing to perform it.

You are not just surviving anymore.
You are rising—
from the inside out.

You've learned to speak your name
with reverence.
To breathe through the storms
without waiting for rescue.
To trust your own voice
after silence tried to steal it.

You've made peace
with a life that looks nothing like you planned—
and still, you're building something beautiful.

You've become your own safe place.
Your own steady ground.
Your own reminder that love didn't end—
it just found new roots
inside of you.

So if no one else says it,
let me say it here:

I see the woman you've become.
And she is powerful.
Not because she never broke—
but because she put herself back together
in a way that no one else could.

You are not who you were before your loss.
And you don't need to be.

And if you've ever curled up in bed,
reaching for a ghost— in the middle of the night.
Half-expecting to lose them again
even though they're already gone.
Not because you believe they're really there,
but because your body remembers
how it felt when they were—
then you know.
You know the ache of loving someone
who isn't coming back.
You know the emptiness of a space
where warmth once lived.
You know what it means
to fall asleep beside silence,
and still wake up with love in your heart.

That kind of love doesn't end.
It transforms.
It teaches you how to be your own comfort.
Your own anchor.
Your own safe place
when the bed feels too big
and the world feels too quiet.

And if you're still reaching—
not to hold on,
but to remember—
then I see you.
And you are not alone.

That kind of grief—
it doesn't just echo.
It aches.

You've learned to live
with an empty pillow,
one vanity,
folding laundry that's only yours and kids.
You've held conversations in your head
just to feel a little less alone.

You didn't choose this.
But you're surviving it.
And there's a kind of quiet heroism in that.

So don't let anyone make you feel
like "being used to it" means it hurts less.
It just means you've grown strong enough
to sit beside the ache
and still wake up
with a heart that hopes.

Even if the space beside you is still empty tonight—
you are still here.
Still becoming.
And that is a sacred kind of defiance.

You are rooted now—
not in what you lost,
but in what you've risen from.

And that?
That is a kind of strength
the world doesn't always recognize...
but will never be able to take from you.

That—right there—is the truth of a warrior heart.
A widow's heart.

You didn't choose this pain.
But you're choosing what to do with it.

And yes,
both giving up and keep going are hard.

But only one of them
carries the chance of hope.
Only one leads you to the other side
where peace might just be waiting—
with sunlight warm enough
to remind you
you're still alive.
Still becoming.

You may not have asked for this new life,
but you are shaping it into something
no one else could:

And maybe years from now,
when I open the bag of gummy bears and smile,
it won't just be for the taste.
It'll be for the memory.
The way love lingers—
in flavors, in glances,
in all the quiet ways he once made me feel seen.

"That's the part of love
they can never take."

Rebuilding wasn't hopeful.
It was heavy.
It was painful in ways I still don't know how to name.

There was no clear vision.
No inspiration boards, no joyful planning.
Just blueprints blurred by tears
and decisions made through grief-soaked exhaustion.

Each door handle I had to pick—
felt like betrayal.
Each cabinet style,
each window trim,
each mirror—
a gut-punch reminder
that none of this would bring him back.

Even the room sizes…
they brought me to my knees. I struggled with layout.
Do I keep the same flow?
Do I build something new? Should I use our old foundation—
a cracked but sacred place—
or pour a new one?

That decision alone wrecked me. Because the truth is,
I didn't want either.
I just wanted him.

I didn't want to build again.
I wanted to go back.
But life doesn't offer a rewind button. Only bricks, budgets, and painful
progress.

And before any of that...
there was the demolition. The day the house came down,
I screamed. I sobbed so hard I thought
my heart would give out. I watched every last brick,
every board, every finish crumble—
a slow-motion goodbye
I wasn't ready for.

It wasn't just a house.
It was our home. And watching it fall apart in front of me
felt like losing him all over again.

I'd sit in front of design books,
not because I wanted to,
but because someone told me it was time to choose.
As if choosing a ceiling height
could ever replace the safety I lost
the day mine collapsed.

Every step felt like a lie.
I was building a life
I didn't even know anymore.

I just wanted to go back to the life that I knew.

I hated it.

I hated that I had to do it.
I hated that I had to be the one making choices
he should have been here for.
I hated the silence in showrooms,
the pit in my stomach when someone asked,
"Do you have a specific style you're going for?"

Yes.
It was called ours.
And it burned.

But we do it.
Not because it's easy—
but because we have no other choice.

A life that honors what was lost
and still dares to rise anyway.

You are already walking that bridge
between survival and becoming.

Continue to rise, finish building a life
for the woman who keeps trying,
even when it's hard.

Because maybe—just maybe—
peace is closer than you think.

Delilah Klug

I am no longer just surviving.
I am no longer carrying life only in pieces.

I am learning to rest in the wholeness of who I've become—
rooted in peace,
rooted in grace,
rooted in love that has carried me through.

I am not who I was before the fire.
I am not even the woman I was in survival.

I am the woman who rose in the aftermath,
who gathered the pieces,
who planted roots in the very ground
that tried to bury her.

The storms may come,
the ache may linger,
but my roots are steady now.

And for the first time in a long time,
I am not afraid of the quiet.
Because the quiet has shown me—
I am enough.
I am safe.
I am home.

I am still here—
not because it was easy,
not because it was graceful,
but because my roots grew deeper than the ruin.

Each and every scar
I will wear like a badge of honor—
proof of the battles I survived.

And if there's one truth I know now, it is this:
I may bend.
I may break open.
I may ache for what was.
But I will not be uprooted.

I am rooted in me.

Letter from My Future Self

Dear Me,

I know you're tired of being the strong one.

I remember the nights you stayed awake wondering if it would always hurt this much.
If the world would ever stop expecting you to carry everything—
the grief, the kids, the silence, the decisions,
the pressure to look like you're okay
when nothing about this life has felt okay since the day you lost him.

I know what it's like to feel invisible in a room full of people.
To hear advice from people who have no idea what it took
to wake up that morning.
To feed your babies.
To answer the phone.
To choose not to disappear.

But here's what I need you to know:

You didn't fail.

Not when you broke down in the bathroom.
Not when you screamed into a pillow after holding it together all day.
Not when you questioned God.
Not even when you wished for the pain to stop—permanently.

You didn't fail.

You were human.
And grief—real grief—rewrites everything.
It stripped you bare.
Took what you loved and left you to rebuild with hands still shaking.
You were grieving a man, a marriage, a future, a home,
your children's future with their father,
and a version of yourself that would never come back.
Of course you felt lost.
Of course you still do, some days.

But here's what you couldn't see yet:

Every day you kept breathing was a declaration.
Every boundary you set was grace.
Every tear you shed was evidence of how deeply you loved.
Every time you chose to show up—for your kids, for yourself—was an
act of radical grace.

You thought you were surviving.
But you were becoming.

And now, here I am—
A woman who no longer apologizes for her grief.
A woman who no longer explains her softness or her silence.
A woman who doesn't shrink herself to be palatable.
Who holds her own hand when no one else shows up.
Who trusts her instincts, even when no one claps for her strength.

You won't always feel this raw.

One day you'll laugh again, and it won't be forced.
You'll wake up and not feel the weight before your eyes even open.
You'll create new memories, not to replace the old ones—but to live
alongside them.

There will be a moment—quiet, sacred—where you'll feel proud.
Not because you conquered grief,
but because you stopped pretending you had to.

You'll stop performing healing.
And you'll start living.

Not in spite of the past.
But because of how it shaped you.

You'll still carry him.
Still ache sometimes.
But you won't feel like you're drowning anymore.

You'll have become someone even he would be proud of—
Not because you moved on,
but because you moved forward
and kept your heart intact.

You're not just surviving.
You are rebuilding a life with roots that reach deeper than the pain.

So take your time.
Fall apart when you need to.
And rise when you're ready.

You don't owe the world a polished version of your pain.
You only owe yourself the honesty of where you are.

I'm waiting for you.
And I promise—
you're going to be so proud of the woman you become.

You're not just surviving.
You are learning to live again—
with roots steady enough to hold you,
and hope strong enough to carry you forward.

You are growing into a life that feels safe again,
a life where your heart can breathe,
and your love can keep on living.

You are becoming—
a woman who carries her story with strength,
her love with honor,
and her future with open hands.

And that future is already waiting for you.

—Your Future Self

The Body Remembers

Grief doesn't just break your heart.
It breaks your body, too.

No one told me
that my chest would physically ache,
that my breath would shorten
at random times of day.
That silence would press against my lungs
like a weight.

No one told me
that my muscles would stay tense
for months,
that my jaw would stay clenched
from holding back tears
I didn't even know were still there.

I was tired.
Bone tired.
Soul tired.
Tired in a way that sleep couldn't fix.

I didn't recognize my own reflection.
My eyes were hollow.
My skin dull.
My smile forced—
when it appeared at all.

Grief lived in my stomach.
In my shoulders.
In the headaches that pulsed
without warning.

It lived in the way I flinched
when someone said his name too softly.
In the way I startled
at noises that used to be background.
In the way my hands shook
when I tried to write
what I couldn't say.

The body remembers what the heart cannot say out loud.
It carries the tension of every goodbye,
the echo of every almost,
the weight of every "are you okay?"
when you're barely standing.

And still—
somehow—
this body kept going.

Bruised.
Scared.
Cut.
Tired.
But standing.

Because even when the soul felt too heavy, my body carried me here.
And that, too, is survival.

Delilah Klug

To the Widow Who's Still Here

You are not just surviving.
You are carrying a love that didn't end—
and a strength you never asked for,
but now wear like a quiet crown.

This life looks nothing like you planned.
And still, here you are.
Rebuilding.
Becoming.
Breathing.

There is no rulebook for this kind of grief.
Only the rhythm of your own heartbeat—
one that carries sorrow,
memory,
grace,
and grit
all at once.

So if no one has told you lately:

You are doing so much better than you think.
You are allowed to take your time.
You are allowed to fall apart and start again.
I walk this journey with you.

Let this be your reminder
that you're not too broken.
You are living through the unimaginable
with more courage than most people will ever understand.

This book began with grief.
But it ends with you—
still breathing,
still loving,
still becoming.

For every widow still standing—
your story matters.
Your love remains.

Life let us down, it changed everything.
But it didn't win.

I am still here.
Still becoming.
Still carrying what matters most—
in my soul,
in my spirit,
with a widow's heartbeat
that continues.

ABOUT THE AUTHOR

Delilah Klug is a widow and mother who writes with raw honesty and unwavering grace. After losing her husband in a devastating house fire, she was left with two children, no home, and a grief no one could prepare her for. Out of that heartbreak, she began putting words to the pain, shaping survival into pages of truth.

Her writing isn't about easy answers—it's about offering a hand to hold and a voice that says, *"Me too."* She writes for the widows who were told to "stay strong," for the mothers who held their families together while breaking inside, and for the women who are still crawling through the dark.

Delilah is the author of *Grief Changed Me: So did Grace* and *Grief Changed Me : A Widow's Heartbeat.*

Her books are written in memory of her husband, Dustin Klug— because even in loss, a widow's heartbeat carries on. Softly, quietly, hope whispers too. May you hear it when you need it most.